NEW DIRECTIONS FOR PROGRAM EVALUATION
A Publication of the American Evaluation Association

William R. Shadish, *Memphis State University*
EDITOR-IN-CHIEF

Critically Evaluating the Role of Experiments

Kendon J. Conrad
Department of Veterans Affairs and
University of Illinois at Chicago

EDITOR

Number 63, Fall 1994

JOSSEY-BASS PUBLISHERS
San Francisco

CRITICALLY EVALUATING THE ROLE OF EXPERIMENTS
Kendon J. Conrad (ed.)
New Directions for Program Evaluation, no. 63
William R. Shadish, Editor-in-Chief

Microfilm copies of issues and articles are available in 16mm and 35mm, as well as microfiche in 105mm, through University Microfilms Inc., 300 North Zeeb Road, Ann Arbor, Michigan 48106-1346.

LC 85-644749   ISSN 0164-7989   ISBN 0-7879-9992-X

NEW DIRECTIONS FOR PROGRAM EVALUATION is part of The Jossey-Bass Education Series and is published quarterly by Jossey-Bass Inc., Publishers, 350 Sansome Street, San Francisco, California 94104-1342.

Subscriptions for 1994 cost $54.00 for individuals and $75.00 for institutions, agencies, and libraries.

EDITORIAL CORRESPONDENCE should be sent to the Editor-in-Chief, William R. Shadish, Department of Psychology, Memphis State University, Memphis, Tennessee 38152.

Manufactured in the United States of America. Nearly all Jossey-Bass books, jackets, and periodicals are printed on recycled paper that contains at least 50 percent recycled waste, including 10 percent postconsumer waste. Many of our materials are also printed with vegetable-based inks; during the printing process, these inks emit fewer volatile organic compounds (VOCs) than petroleum-based inks. VOCs contribute to the formation of smog.

EDITORIAL POLICY AND PROCEDURES

NEW DIRECTIONS FOR PROGRAM EVALUATION (NDPE), a quarterly sourcebook, is an official publication of the American Evaluation Association. NDPE publishes empirical, methodological, and theoretical works on all aspects of evaluation and related fields. Substantive areas may include any program, field, or issue with which evaluation is concerned, such as government performance, tax policy, energy, environment, mental health, education, job training, medicine, and public health. Also included are such topics as product evaluation, personnel evaluation, policy analysis, and technology assessment. In all cases, the focus on evaluation is more important than the substantive topics. We are particularly interested in encouraging a diversity of evaluation perspectives and experiences and in expanding the boundaries of our field beyond the evaluation of social programs.

NDPE does not consider or publish unsolicited single manuscripts. Each issue of NDPE is devoted to a single topic, with contributions solicited, organized, reviewed, and edited by a guest editor. Issues may take any of several forms, such as a series of related chapters, a debate, or a long article followed by brief critical commentaries. In all cases, the proposals must follow a specific format, which can be obtained from the editor-in-chief. These proposals are sent to members of the editorial board and to relevant substantive experts for peer review. The process may result in acceptance, a recommendation to revise and resubmit, or rejection. However, NDPE is committed to working constructively with potential guest editors to help them develop acceptable proposals.

Lois-ellin Datta, Editor-in-Chief
P.O. Box 383768
Waikoloa, HI 96738

Jennifer C. Greene, Associate Editor
Department of Human Service Studies
Cornell University
Ithaca, NY 14853-4401

Gary Henry, Associate Editor
Public Administration and Urban Studies
Georgia State University
Atlanta, GA 30302-4039

CONTENTS

EDITOR'S NOTES

This issue of *New Directions for Program Evaluation* principally stems from a cooperative agreement project funded by the National Institute on Alcohol Abuse and Alcoholism (NIAAA) in cooperation with the National Institute on Drug Abuse (NIDA). This cooperative agreement involved fourteen projects, ten of which began with randomized experimental designs, that is, randomized clinical trials; the other four were quasi-experiments.

As a principal investigator on one of these projects, I coedited a book (Conrad, Hultman, and Lyons, 1993) that describes the theory underlying each project and the implementation issues that arose during the projects. In editing these chapters, we noticed that virtually all of the projects were experiencing problems implementing their research studies in community-based treatment programs. The randomized experiments seemed to have somewhat greater problems due to the greater control needed for randomization with its attendant focus on ensuring good internal validity.

In editing our book, we found that the implementation aspects of experimentation dominated the discussions of threats to validity. How common, plausible, and virulent were threats that arose because of implementation problems? How important were threats to construct validity and external validity when there were strong reactions to the experiment that seemed to change the phenomena being studied and make them atypical of the world outside the experiment? More generally, what did these threats mean for community-based experiments? As Berk and others (1985) noted, "We now know that the implementation of proper experimental procedures is at least as important as the design of experiments" (p. 397).

Given this interest, I asked whether any of the members of the NIAAA cooperative agreement would be interested in contributing chapters that would describe their implementation problems in greater depth and detail. Some were, and those papers that were most germane are presented here. Subsequently, I asked the leadership of the NIAAA cooperative agreement if they would provide their perspective on these issues and discuss how the problems that arose were addressed and what could be done to improve future studies of this type. Robert G. Orwin, David S. Cordray, and Robert B. Huebner agreed to do so. I then recruited Michael L. Dennis and Robert F. Boruch to provide a more general discussion of "tricks of the trade" that are useful in implementing community-based experiments. Finally, I asked David M. Fetterman, long a critic of experimentation, to write an afterword for the volume from a qualitative perspective.

Therefore, this issue begins with a chapter by Karen M. Conrad and me that attempts an overview of threats to validity that can, and often do, arise in the real world of experimentation. These threats may not be new to experienced experimenters. However, we believe that this discussion is important because most experiments are conducted by principal investigators who have not previously conducted experiments (Dennis and Boruch, this volume). This chapter also sets the stage for the ensuing presentations of validity threats in actual experiments as well as for discussions of ways to avoid, reduce, or remove threats. In this chapter, the threats are presented with an unusual focus on construct validity. It is organized using Cronbach's UTOS paradigm (Cronbach, 1982), a paradigm that is generally unfamiliar to evaluators (Shadish and Epstein, 1987). The construct validity perspective does not rely on experiments for rigor but emphasizes replicability instead.

Joel A. Devine, James D. Wright, and Laurie M. Joyner then present an engaging discussion of the motives and methods involved in subverting random assignment to the point that their experiment became, in reality, a quasi-experiment. For example, in their study, issues of program control and clinical judgment resulted in "creaming" clients differentially into the experimental group but not into the control group, resulting in a "lifeboat" effect where women and children were rescued into the experimental group.

Joseph E. Schumacher, Jesse B. Milby, James M. Raczynski, Molly Engle, Ellen S. Caldwell, and James A. Carr illustrate the nature and causes of demoralization and other threats in a randomized experiment and discuss how demoralization forced changes in the implementation of the experimental and control groups. Then Sally J. Stevens discusses the implementation of three randomized experiments that shared common problems such as the ethical concerns of program staff, "intervention slippage," and the reactions of referring agencies to the research demonstration. She also presents the strategies that were developed to deal with these issues.

Through interviews with subjects, staff, and community providers, Julie A. Lam, Stephanie Wilson Hartwell, and James F. Jekel reveal reactions to random assignment that created misgivings and bad feelings in their project in New Haven, Connecticut. Despite the perceived problems, they conclude that randomization was successful and not a significant threat to the validity of the findings. However, Paul Johnston and Patrick Swift, who conducted the qualitative component of the New Haven study, disagree with this conclusion; their chapter explains this disagreement, chiefly from a qualitative perspective.

I should note that the fourteen NIAAA cooperative agreement sites and the national evaluation team met two or three times in each of the three years of the project. These meetings were exceptionally constructive and synergistic in promoting program and research collaboration and improvement. The national evaluation team is to be commended for promoting the spirit of open interchange that led to the frank discussion of the many sensitive topics included here and in Conrad, Hultman, and Lyons (1993). The projects themselves are to be commended for maintaining a constructive, self-critical dialogue that brought these tough issues to light.

I am most grateful to William Shadish for his insightful reviews and patience in helping me to develop this volume. He and the *New Directions for Program Evaluation* editorial board were very helpful in their review of our overview of construct validity threats. Of course, we assume full responsibility for its shortcomings. Jack Goldberg, James Heckman, John Lyons, Larry Manheim, Charles Reichardt, and the contributors to this issue provided useful comments at various points along the way. I am also grateful to Evert Cuesta for editorial assistance and to Danette Hopkins-Bey for manuscript preparation assistance.

Kendon J. Conrad
Editor

References

Berk, R. A., and others. "Social Policy Experimentation: A Position Paper." *Evaluation Review,* 1985, *9* (4), 387–429.

Conrad, K. J., Hultman, C. I., and Lyons, J. S. "Treatment of the Chemically Dependent Homeless: Theory and Implementation in Fourteen American Projects." *Alcoholism Treatment Quarterly,* 1993, *10* (3–4).

Cronbach, L. J. *Designing Evaluations of Educational and Social Programs.* San Francisco: Jossey-Bass, 1982.

Shadish, W. R., and Epstein, R. "Patterns of Program Evaluation Practice among Members of the Evaluation Research Society and Evaluation Network." *Evaluation Review,* 1987, *11* (3), 555–590.

KENDON J. CONRAD is associate director of the Midwest Center for Health Services and Policy Research at Hines VA Hospital. He is also associate professor at the University of Illinois School of Public Health, where he is associate director of the Center for Health Services Research.

The focus on internal validity in randomized experiments can be misguided if construct validity is neglected. This chapter provides an overview of construct validity threats in randomized experiments and discusses some implications of reducing these threats for future evaluations.

Reassessing Validity Threats in Experiments: Focus on Construct Validity

Kendon J. Conrad, Karen M. Conrad

The randomized experiment has shown great success in answering key scientific questions. A strength of randomized experiments is the comparison of two or more theoretically equal groups consisting of a control or placebo versus a treatment or treatments of interest. When the conditions are maintained for a valid comparison of the control versus treatment groups, the experiment can be a powerful instrument for answering causal questions.

Among those who conduct program evaluations, however, serious questions have arisen about the goals and methods (Ashery and McAuliffe, 1992; Chen and Rossi, 1983; Cronbach, 1982; Heckman, 1992; White and Weidman, 1983) and aspects of the findings (Cook, 1993; Cronbach, 1982; Hennessy and Hennessy, 1990; Levitan, 1992) of randomized experiments in studies of social and health programs. Even strong proponents of randomization and field experimentation stress that experiments in field settings break down, are difficult to implement, and require strong justification, pilot-testing, negotiations, contingency plans, education of participants, and so on (Boruch and Wothke, 1985; Dennis and Boruch, this volume; Orwin, Cordray, and Huebner, this volume).

The applicability of the results of experiments in improving programs and their outcomes is probably one key test of their usefulness. In this regard, Brekke (1988) noted, "Studies have shown that community support programs are more effective in treating the chronic mentally ill than traditional forms of aftercare. Yet an analysis of 33 controlled studies of community support programs reveals that almost no systematic empirical knowledge exists about their implementation, including the kinds of treatment they deliver, how they can be replicated, or what ingredients account for their success" (p. 946). Based on evidence such as this and other sources too numerous to list here, this chapter proposes that there is insufficient appreciation, at least in some circles, for the limits of the randomized experiment as a research method, and a concurrent lack of attention to other important areas and types of research. Therefore, it is important to reexamine the role and, especially, the limitations of experiments. The experiment is designed to ensure internal validity. The thesis of this chapter is that a focus on internal validity is misguided if construct validity is neglected. Therefore, this chapter is designed to provide an overview of construct validity threats that may present problems in experiments. The point is not to attack the experiment as a method and suggest that some other method is superior. We recognize that other methods have many of these same problems or other peculiar problems. The purpose is to help remove any false sense that experiments are inherently superior and to articulate some of the challenges to be overcome in conducting experiments. The focus on the limitations of experiments is intended to help researchers use experiments in the right situations, avoid pitfalls, improve the implementation of experiments, and use them more appropriately in conjunction with other methods.

We will attempt to integrate the works on validity threats presented mainly by Campbell and Stanley (1963), Cook and Campbell (1979), and Cronbach (1982). Although the classic books on threats to validity (Campbell and Stanley, 1963; Cook and Campbell, 1979) discuss threats to all types of validity, they tend to emphasize internal validity threats to causal inference in experiments and quasi-experiments. Additionally, as Cronbach pointed out, they tended to limit internal generalization (statistical conclusion validity) to generalization over persons (units) only. The present discussion will stress the threats to construct validity that remain when the focus of the study is on internal validity. Also, it will examine how the threats operate not only over units but also over treatments, observations, and settings. Finally, the chapter will discuss how a greater emphasis on construct validity can improve program evaluations.

Review of the Role of the Experiment: Internal Validity

Experiments exist to facilitate causal inference (Cook and Campbell, 1979). They are designed to promote internal validity—the validity of the causal hypothesis concerning whether A makes a difference in B "in this specific experimental instance" (Campbell and Stanley, 1963, p. 5). In Cronbach's terms, did this particular treatment (t) make a difference as measured on this particular observation (o) with this particular unit (u) in this setting (S)? (Note: Lowercase denotes the study sample, uppercase the study population; the S is capitalized because the sample and study population are the same.) To

Campbell and Stanley, external validity concerned generalization from the study to the population of interest, and it was of secondary importance to internal validity in experimental work.

The hallmark of Campbell and Stanley is the primacy of internal validity, which they refer to as the "sine qua non" (1963, p. 5). That is, if you cannot infer that A caused B in the study, what is the use of trying to generalize to the population of interest? However, these authors did note that "the selection of designs strong in both types of validity is obviously our ideal" (p. 5). Furthermore, Cook and Campbell noted, "In the end, however, each investigator has to try to design research which maximizes all kinds of validity and, if he or she decides to place a primacy on internal validity, this cannot be allowed to trivialize the research" (p. 91).

An overemphasis on internal validity can be misguided if construct validity is neglected. For example, the construct validity of the treatment (the cause) is not addressed in classic randomized experiments (Campbell and Stanley, 1963). As Cronbach noted, "the conclusion capable of having internal validity in Campbell's sense is, 'Something made a difference.' Cook and Campbell (1979) are careful to say that labeling the cause raises a question of construct validity and that the interpretation cannot be purely deductive. *Identifying* the cause is not part of the claim for internal validity" (1982, p. 130).

Cronbach emphasized that in applied settings where there are many constructs interacting in a complex network of cause and effect, it is necessary to clarify the nature of the constructs and their relationships. To Cronbach, the important thing was not the causal inference (A causes B in this sample); rather, it concerns the reproducibility of results from one sample of units (u), treatments (t), and observations (o) to other samples within the populations of units (U), treatments (T), and observations (O); and, ultimately, to other populations (UTOS) of units, treatments, observations, and settings. Therefore, the construct validity of the treatment (that is, the cause) is a crucial concern, as is the construct validity of the unit, observation, and setting. Along with others (see Messick, 1989, for a review), Cronbach concluded that "all validation is one" (Messick, 1989, p. 18), where the "one" is construct validity.

Construct Validity

As an important definitional note, Cronbach did not define internal and external validity in the same way as did Campbell and colleagues. To Cronbach, internal validity is concerned with the reproducibility of the results of a study. Therefore, if an effect is observed, will this effect be observed upon replication of the study? In the true experiment, with its emphasis on internal validity, there is a tendency to focus on the pre- and posttreatment observation of the units while leaving the cause as a black box. However, when researchers are concerned with replication, there is also a need to be concerned with causes (treatments), their observation, and the setting that influences them. When we study complex social programs, the understanding of treatment, its implementation, its observation, and its setting is important for replication of the cause construct.

A focus on the cause is essential because the cause precedes the effect. Therefore, by gaining a reliable understanding of the cause, we can improve our ability to manipulate it and replicate it. With this ability, we can more reliably produce the desired effect.

Regarding external validity, extrapolation of the construct beyond the study population to other populations is still an issue of construct validity. Therefore, external validity is simply the construct validity of the results of the study sample (utoS) generalized to the study population (UTOS), which is then generalized to other populations (*UTOS). "External" construct validity also concerns whether the sample of units (u), treatments (t), observations (o), and Setting (S) accurately match or represent the population of Units (U), Treatments (T), Observations (O), and Setting (S), and other populations of *U, *T, *O, and *S. For example, if office workers (u) at a New York City insurance company are studied, how well do they represent the construct "office workers at New York City insurance companies" (U) or "other populations of office workers" (*U)? If a five-day smoking cessation program given by a religious organization (t) is studied, how well does it represent the construct "five-day smoking cessation programs given by religious groups" (T) or "other kinds of smoking cessation programs" (*T)? If the Alcohol Dependence Scale (o) interview is used as an observation of "alcohol consumption," how well does it represent or correlate with other interview measures of alcohol consumption (O) or with measures using different methods such as urine toxicology tests, blood tests, reports of family members, or paper and pencil self-reports (*O)? If a study is done in New York City (S), how well does it represent similar studies done in other places (*S)? Again, the key to assessing construct validity is replication of expected relationships.

Construct validity is usually not as great a problem when constructs are stable, concrete, low in variance, and few in number; that is, they change very slowly over time, have material characteristics, and are similar across populations; for example, studies of fertilizer and plants or drugs and animals deal with *relatively* stable phenomena. To illustrate, Heckman (1992) makes the point that "The Fisher model may be ideal for the study of fertilizer treatments on crop yields. Plots of ground do not respond to anticipated treatments of fertilizer, nor can they excuse themselves from being treated" (p. 215). In contrast, human subjects are purposive, reactive, and more varied. This reactivity and variability presents a major hurdle to generalization from the typical community-based experiment.

Construct Validity Threats to Units, Treatments, Observations, and Settings

This section presents a general overview of the construct validity issues that arise in experiments. It is organized in four sections addressing units, treatments, observations, and settings to emphasize the importance of considering threats to each of these components of experiments. We provide examples or refer to cases in the literature, or refer to the other chapters in this issue so that the reader may get a stronger intuitive sense of how the threats work in real-world experiments. Because of space limitations, the list of threats covered here is not exhaustive, but we did try to emphasize those we thought were most important. Although the discussion is a critique of experiments, many of the threats are plausible in other research designs as well. As Cronbach (1982) noted, a discussion of this type "rarely signals what is right to do, but it can warn against numerous shortsighted courses of action. Replacing unwarranted certainty with uncertainty is a contribution" (p. 175).

Threats to the Construct Validity of the Unit. By *unit* we mean the subject of the study. These may be human cells, rats, human beings, employee fitness centers, worksites, cities, countries, and so on. Researchers obtain a sample of units for the study that is intended to represent the population of interest. To allow at least some generalizability, it is common to strictly define the target population to be studied.

Unit of Analysis. Choosing the wrong unit of analysis is a construct validity threat because we study one unit construct, such as a person, but we generalize to another unit construct, such as a project, worksite, or school (Whiting-O'Keefe, Henke, and Simborg, 1984; Koepke and Flay, 1989). Typically, the individual has been the unit of analysis in program evaluation studies. More recently we are beginning to see the program also treated as the unit of analysis (Wheat and others, 1992; Conrad, Hughes, Hanrahan, and Wang, 1993). The key issue here is generalization. For example, it is usually of questionable validity to generalize to worksite smoking cessation programs from the units (u) studied at one worksite smoking cessation project.

Units must be independent of each other. In biomedical studies, this principle is clear and is rarely violated. For example, a drug is given to one person and a placebo to the second person. A researcher would not observe the effect by taking one hundred blood samples from each person and calling the blood sample the unit of analysis. Doing so would provide an n of one hundred cases, which would overrepresent the power of the analysis.

In program evaluation, however, it is common to administer the experimental treatment at one worksite or school or agency, then sample one hundred individuals at this site, call the individual the unit, and then generalize to the program (Whiting-O'Keefe, Henke, and Simborg, 1984). Just as one hundred blood samples taken from the same person are not independent, neither are one hundred workers from the same site totally independent; they all share one emanation of the experimental treatment and a common environment. Sampling units from multiple treatments is needed to improve the generalizability of both unit and treatment constructs, and statistics are now available to account for the clustering of units within treatments (Goldstein, 1987).

Representativeness of the Unit Construct. The construct validity of the unit is usually threatened when high percentages of eligible clients who are in the target population fail or refuse to participate in the study (Devine, Wright, and Joyner, this volume; Dennis and Boruch, this volume). For example, Ashery and McAuliffe (1992) discuss this problem in a study in which only 4 percent of 2,000 persons originally responding were actually randomized into the study. Also, Howard, Cox, and Saunders (1989) discuss this issue in a study that randomized 9 percent of 6,000 prospective subjects. With selected samples, the generalizability of the study subjects to the unit construct of interest may be severely compromised.

The unit construct can be further distorted when participants in baseline measurement are lost to follow-up (attrition from measurement). This is especially a problem in experiments when the attrition differs between the groups (Schumacher and others, this volume). For example, when the control group is angry about being denied the preferred experimental treatment, some may refuse to cooperate in the research.

Furthermore, the unit construct of interest is people in treatment versus those in control. In some cases, subjects will object to their assignment, whether treatment or control, and will not show up for the program. For example, of the heroin addicts assigned to an experimental program, 24 percent never showed up and thus were actually more typical of the control group unit construct (see Bloom, 1984, for a discussion and proposed solution).

In other cases, the service providers will decide that the random assignment is inappropriate for certain clients and will change the assignment based on clinical needs (Schumacher and others, this volume). In the chapter by Devine, Wright, and Joyner (this volume), women were found to be more than three times as likely to go into the experimental group as men. The investigators were concerned, quite reasonably, that this was not a random occurrence, but that randomization status was changed, especially for women who had greater need for the more intense experimental treatment. Although the researchers found the groups to be equivalent on most characteristics at baseline, there is no telling what effect the large gender nonequivalence would have on outcomes (unit/treatment interaction). In one of the few studies where the failure of intended random assignment was studied, Berk, Smyth, and Sherman (1988) found that 18 percent of the intended random assignments had been changed because the service providers judged them to be inappropriate. The authors estimated that had these changes not been made, the observed effect would have been double.

Reactions to the Experiment. Because people are conscious and reactive, when we conduct social experiments, we usually give up a key aspect of experiments as they are implemented in agricultural and biomedical settings—the double blind. When subjects are aware of the discrepancy between treatment and control conditions, they may no longer behave as treatment and control subjects would behave if there were only a treatment condition or only a control condition. A basic threat to the construct validity of research units is that people who are being studied and know they are being studied behave differently from those not being studied or who do not know they are being studied. For example, in the homeless demonstrations (Orwin, Cordray, and Huebner, this volume), the unit construct of interest was "homeless substance abusers," but the actual unit construct turned out to be "homeless substance abusers who were aware of being randomized to either an experimental or a control condition."

Competition and Demoralization. The competition engendered by the control versus treatment comparisons in randomized experiments can threaten the validity of the unit construct in both the control and intervention group. For example, workers in the control group may try to compensate for their lack of "special" treatment and try harder, especially if they think the experimental intervention is a threat to their jobs (this is known as the John Henry effect). Other subjects may become demoralized and slack off because they resent not getting the "new, improved" experimental treatment. They may play games of minimal involvement that consist of their producing a minimally acceptable performance, getting their subject fee, and leaving as soon as possible (Argyris, 1980). Still other subjects may try to second-guess the researcher and give the "best" or "correct" responses.

Ethical Issues. Clients may be offended by the usurpation of their usual choices or what they perceive as rights. Even under conditions of scarcity, some subjects will insist that first-come should be first-served rather than allocated on a random basis. Human beings recognize when they are denied their accustomed choices and may react to this treatment with anger and rebellion (Lam, Hartwell, and Jekel, this volume). Such reactions can cause demoralization and diminish the effectiveness of customary care (Schumacher and others, this volume).

As researchers, we point out that they consented to the random assignment, but some subjects may do so only for the opportunity to obtain the scarce resource to which they feel they are entitled. Once this opportunity has been closed, they feel no obligation to continue serving as controls. In fact, the experimental treatment could create a new standard of care that both subjects and customary providers work to obtain (Stevens, this volume).

Construct Validity of the Treatment. Traditionally, in agriculture and many biomedical applications, treatment was relatively well-specified and stable, as in fertilizer and drug trials. Because experimental research has grown out of disciplines where constructs are relatively stable, we tend to think of generalizing in terms of study subjects (units). A key point in Cronbach is that, like the units, the treatments, observations, and settings are also just samples of larger populations of treatments, observations, and settings. Therefore, we must also ask, How representative is the study sample of treatments, observations, and the setting to the populations of treatments, observations, and settings?

Cronbach emphasized that if we study only a single example of the treatment, it is unlikely that this will adequately represent the population of treatments. Furthermore, strict standardization of the treatment in multisite applications will restrict its generalizability and adaptability.

Mono-Operation Bias. When the program is represented by one treatment modality (one kind of treatment, one program leader), mono-operation bias of the treatment can be a threat. In other words, when we study a single example of the treatment, it can never be clear that the construct represented by *A* caused *B* because there are many other constructs (causes) accompanying *A* that may have contributed to or detracted from *B* (the effect). For example, in worksite health promotion research, these other constructs (also referred to as random irrelevancies by Cook and Campbell, 1979) include such factors as the personality of the program leader, corporate policy, the company culture, and management support for the program. Using one individual or one strictly delineated script, or one type of equipment, furniture, room, and so on, may help standardize the treatment, but at the same time it restricts construct (external) validity.

Unrepresentative Sample of Treatments. When studies of the population of treatments have not been done (the usual case), a certain subclass of the treatment may come to represent the entire population. This was probably the case in the field of adult day care, where the experiments were all performed on expensive health model centers that represented less than 10 percent of the population of centers (Conrad, Hughes, Hanrahan, and Wang, 1993). Until a study of the entire population of adult day care centers was done, people tended to generalize to all of adult day care, probably just because it was unclear that subclasses existed.

As another example, Heckman (1992) describes an experiment by the Manpower Demonstration Research Corporation (MDRC) in which 90 percent of the eligible training centers refused to participate. The major reasons for refusal included the ethical and public relations implications of random assignment in denial of services to controls and the potential negative effect of creation of a control group on the achievement of client recruitment goals. In this example, it is most likely that the participating centers were uncharacteristic of centers in general. A descriptive study of the population of centers would have been most helpful in clarifying the limits of generalizability.

Program Staff Reactions. Another key feature of the experiment is the experimenter's ability to manipulate the treatment. In agricultural and biomedical experiments when treatments are stable and passive, the researcher can assume that randomization itself did not alter the program being studied (Heckman, 1992). However, in social and health services research, the treatments are influenced by the people delivering them (program staff reactions). Like the subjects of the study, program staff are also aware of their participation in the study and may alter the treatment or control in subtle ways in reaction to the research. In these settings, standardization of treatment and control conditions can be very problematical.

Program staff may view random assignment as unfair to clients who do not get the "new, improved" program but who they believe could benefit from it. Like study subjects, the control and experimental program implementers can experience resentful demoralization or compensatory rivalry. Also, the experimenters themselves can experience qualms about assigning needy subjects to a control condition (Lam, Hartwell, and Jekel, this volume).

We would expect that people delivering a new, experimental treatment would be more excited about the program and motivated to prove that it works. Additionally, the researchers may have chosen program personnel who have special training, skills, and interests that will not be so readily available when the new treatment is attempted at other sites (Berk, Smyth, and Sherman, 1988; McAuliffe and Ashery, 1993). If certain providers are chosen by the researchers because they will implement the treatment "correctly," this can reduce the construct validity (generalizability) of the treatment to the customary providers.

Moreover, when we standardize a treatment in order to clarify its generalizability, this can generate resentment in the customary providers who have been "volunteered" but who believe in doing things their own way. They may disagree with the standardized version, think it is inappropriate for their population, refuse or be unable to learn new skills or attitudes needed for its implementation, and resent the assumption of control of the treatment by the researchers.

Control Issues. A major obstacle to the construct validity of the treatment may be the inequitable distribution of power in experimental studies of health services (Argyris, 1980; Chubin and Hackett, 1990). When researchers conduct experiments in a rigorous manner to ensure internal validity, they take control of the assignment to treatment and control conditions. Random assignment itself is an atypical, nongeneralizable method that clinicians themselves would rarely, if ever, use. Additionally, the creation of experimental and control groups can create the perception of random misassignment. By this we mean that clinicians perceive that random assignment is resulting in inappropriate clinical assignment.

Perception of Random Misassignment. Because it is often difficult to obtain statistically significant results, researchers feel pressure to make and keep the differences in how experimental and control groups are treated as great as possible. Conversely, service providers feel that clients should be treated equitably and optimally. Therefore, the greater the difference in treatment between groups, the more likely it is for ethical problems to arise for the service providers (see McAuliffe and Ashery, 1993, for a more complete discussion).

Usually, a version of customary care is provided, then it is compared to a high intensity or specialized experimental intervention. When random assignment takes place in this situation, clinical judgment about the most appropriate service package for each individual is absent. In this situation, the random placement of clients into services may be viewed clinically as inappropriate in some cases (Devine, Wright, and Joyner, this volume), with the result that providers and clients may find it difficult to participate in the research and even in the program itself. Therefore, in an effort to create experimental and control groups, the researcher can create a situation that is abnormal (lacking construct validity for the intended normal treatment) and problematical for participants. Lam, Hartwell, and Jekel (this volume) present an excellent example of the reactions of a service provider who has one client who is ready for the enhanced treatment but is assigned to control; then, a client who is seen as not ready is assigned to the treatment group (see also White and Weidman, 1983).

In the chapter by Lam, Hartwell, and Jekel, all clients were judged to be eligible for the intensive treatment, which presented a problem in denying appropriate care to those assigned to the control group. Even if a more complete array of clients is included in the experiment, does the problem still exist? This issue is illustrated in Figure 1.1, where twenty enrolled clients are arrayed on a continuum of need from lowest to highest, and the continuum of care is split into low-intensity customary care and the new, high-intensity experimental care. When the subjects are randomly assigned to customary and experimental conditions, it is likely that five of the low-need clients will be assigned to high-intensity care and five of the high-need clients will be assigned to low-intensity care. If, by chance, randomization does not work, all twenty clients could be misassigned, with ten high-need clients to low-intensity care and ten low-need clients to high-intensity care. Of course, it could happen that the perceived optimal assignment could also occur.

The researchers might argue that we cannot know whether the clinicians' opinions about matching need and care were right; therefore, it is fair to do random assignment. However, even if the clinicians are wrong, they may view the assignment as unfair, inappropriate, or unethical and may try to subvert the experiment. Due to the perception of random misassignment, referral agencies may be reluctant to cooperate. If the clinicians in this example are right, the following may occur: Misassigned clients tend to drop out of treatment more, the ability to observe generalizable main effects is diminished because patients and treatments were poorly matched, and clinicians refuse to support research procedures and findings.

Scarcity. The experimental services should be in scarce supply and remain so in order to avoid perceptions of unfairness in randomly assigning subjects

Figure 1.1. Perception of Random Misassignment

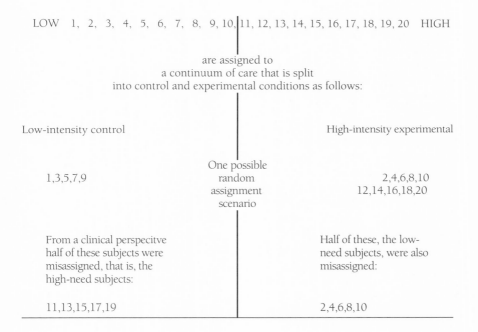

Twenty eligible subjects arranged on a
continuum of need

LOW   1, 2, 3, 4, 5, 6, 7, 8, 9, 10, 11, 12, 13, 14, 15, 16, 17, 18, 19, 20   HIGH

are assigned to
a continuum of care that is split
into control and experimental conditions as follows:

Low-intensity control   High-intensity experimental

1,3,5,7,9

One possible
random
assignment
scenario

2,4,6,8,10
12,14,16,18,20

From a clinical perspecitve
half of these subjects were
misassigned, that is, the
high-need subjects:

Half of these, the low-
need subjects, were also
misassigned:

11,13,15,17,19   2,4,6,8,10

to the control group. It may be perceived as unfair to deny available service generally believed to be beneficial. Remember, we are not talking about new, untested wonder drugs, but about services such as housing, employment counseling, and substance abuse treatment. At the beginning of experiments, the innovation is usually in short supply. However, in order for the random-ized design to work properly, it is important that the treatment differences remain constant throughout the study. However, from the clinical point of view, the experimental program is usually better and creates a new standard of care (Schumacher and others, this volume), which control clinicians and clients subsequently seek or try to develop. For examples, see Stevens (this volume) and White and Weidman (1983). In many cases, improving customary services becomes possible as the study progresses; for example, in studies involving homeless subjects, more low-cost housing is made available through client, staff, and community efforts (Schumacher and others, this volume; Stevens, this volume). The researcher's mandate is to halt this "contamination."

However, as the supply increases, there is an ethical responsibility to give it to everyone who is eligible (Johnston and Swift, this volume, discuss the scarcity issue when the treatment is underused). Researchers also may be tempted to try to standardize the experimental intervention, but if this means limiting its natural development and change over time, then several problems will arise, such as the ethical problem of limiting improvement, limited generalizability to the real world, and resentment from staff and clients.

Inadequate Development or Implementation of the Treatment Construct. When we conceptualize the treatment construct, we do so for a mature, "ideal" program. However, in the real world of demonstration projects, there may not be time to develop this ideal. In the NIAAA research demonstrations (Orwin, Cordray, and Huebner, this volume; Conrad, Hultman, and Lyons, 1993) several of the experimental program administrators complained that three years was not long enough to assess the effects of the programs because it took almost that long to get them running properly (see Schumacher and others, this volume, for a good example). In situations such as these, one could conclude that the program did not work, when actually its effects were not yet observable due to a natural program development process.

An experiment by Kaluzny (1987) illustrates the importance of assessing treatment implementation construct validity of the cause in an education project developed to train workers to reduce their risk of cancer in which no effect was found. Fortunately, the investigators had clear statements of the program's guiding principles and measured how well they were implemented. They found that the intervention program was poorly implemented, as measured by a low "exposure rate" of plant representatives to the various training activities. Less than 50 percent attendance at training and high turnover of trainees resulted in an implementation force that was largely untrained. In addition, the investigators performed qualitative observation of the training sessions and found that training was generally of poor quality. The investigators concluded that there was no effect because the principles of the program were not used to any great extent at the experimental sites.

A related problem is that research demonstrations often involve a sudden infusion of funding that lasts for a short period. When the demonstration funding ends, the innovative projects ends. If the project, even if found to be effective, could not be generated or sustained by its target community, its generalizability is questionable. The foregoing cases imply a need for careful development of a program philosophy, implementation of the program, and monitoring of its implementation before testing its effectiveness with experiments (Conrad and Miller, 1987; see Johnston and Swift, this volume, for an example).

Interaction of Treatments with Other Treatments. This occurs if respondents undergo more than one treatment. In drug studies, it is clear that the observation of the effect of one drug can be confounded when another drug is used. Because many programs such as worksite health promotion offer multiple interventions (for example, weight control, nutrition, exercise) and respondents can participate in more than one intervention at a time, this is a likely threat to the construct validity of any single treatment. It is particularly a threat with comprehensive, multiple-program studies that do not make a distinction between which programs or how many programs an employee attended. A rare exception to this situation occurred in one reported worksite health promotion program (Widman, Wolfe, and Manning, 1987). When the programs were analyzed separately, the stress management program seemed to decrease job satisfaction. On the other hand, the physical conditioning program appeared to increase job satisfaction. Had employees attended both interventions, how would the individual program treatments have interacted to affect the outcome measure? This is another example of the "black box" problem. When sample size permits, it is useful to disaggregate program participants by the types of programs they attended and then to look at interactions.

Inadequate Explanation of Constructs/Lack of Theory. The experiment tests simple theory, that is, *A* causes *B*. Because the construct represented by *A* need not be clearly defined, experiments have generally been inadequate in their ability to specify the complexity and instability of constructs in social settings. In social and health services research, it turns out that there are very few situations where it is possible to test a stable *A* construct's effect on a stable *B* construct. Instead, we have treatment characteristics such as *A1, A2,* and *A3* at level 1 affecting *B1* units while *A1* at level 2, *A4,* and *A5* affect *B2* units. Without understanding the characteristics of *A* and *B*, the knowledge that *A* caused or did not cause *B* gives us little generalizable information; it lacks construct validity. In studies of complex phenomena, the choice of constructs should depend on the result of a conceptual analysis of the essential factors of the constructs and their relationships. Discussion of the conceptual analysis is often lacking in research reports. Also frequently missing is a presentation of the theoretical framework that guided the research (Chen and Rossi, 1983; Hennessy and Hennessy, 1990).

Causal Systems, Feedback Loops, Pressure, and Stages. As we come to understand the complexity of the relationships between programs and outcomes, we may observe that "*A* causes *B* experiments" are misguided because their presumed cause-effect relationships are too close to each other in time and space to represent accurately a long-term, multistage phenomenon. This is the slam-bang model of causation; for example, does a five-day smoking cessation program help people to reduce or quit smoking? Although this is a researchable question, the answer may be misleading when viewed from the systems perspective, where there are feedback loops and a long-term pressure buildup that eventually bring about the effect.

For example, one theory of the modification of addictive behaviors involves progression through five states—precontemplation, contemplation, preparation, action, and maintenance—where individuals typically cycle through the stages several times before getting the addiction under control (Prochaska, DiClemente, and Norcross, 1992). An experiment that tests the effectiveness of a one-shot treatment program in controlling addiction but does not take the stages of recovery into account will observe an effect only for those patients who are at the stage where such a program can be effective in achieving the ultimate goal. Given this system theory, any one-shot program will fail for most addictive behaviors because recovery is an upward spiral where "falling" is natural. An ongoing program helps to reduce the distance of each fall and move each period of recovery to a higher stage of control.

In other words, our focus on "*A* causes *B*," and the use of the experimental method that is so good at addressing this question, may divert us from the more important question of how to understand and influence the system. Given our system theory, doing an experiment to answer the "*A* causes *B*" question means investing a great amount of time, money, and human resources—a large sample of units is needed to observe a small effect, to address what may be a relatively trivial component of the system.

Cronbach (1982) and Heckman (1992) make the point that input-output experiments overlook the fact that many phenomena and the programs designed to address them have distinct stages. To understand overall program effectiveness, it may be necessary to study the implementation and effectiveness of each stage through a series of "short-reach evaluations" (Cronbach, 1982, p. 224). These would be most effective when studying cohorts longitudinally. Heckman (1992) discusses the difficulty involved in randomizing at each stage. Such studies will require conceptualizing our programs as systems and as components of systems. The longitudinal studies involve replication that can focus on the construct validity of utoS.

Appropriateness of the Research Question. The basic research question posed by experiments is "Does *A* cause *B*?" or "Does the program work?" Without some idea of the construct validity of the u, t, o, and S, the answer to this basic science question is merely a historical fact. For example, we observe that our drug abuse treatment program caused a 10 percent reduction in drug use compared to controls. Without a better understanding of the characteristics of the units, treatments, observations, and setting, we have only a vague idea of how to replicate this finding. This is analogous to mixing chemicals to form a new drug, testing the drug, observing an effect, and then realizing that we did not record the nature of the chemicals, their dosage, the nature of the patients, or the conditions under which they were given. Therefore, we may have learned that something was effective, but we have not learned how to duplicate or manipulate that effect—that is, how to make it generalizable.

A basic issue for program evaluation is often the question of improvability. In social and health services, something must be done to address the various problems. Unlike some medical research, such as drug trials, it is more difficult to develop, test, and approve a social intervention before implementation. Programs *must* be implemented. It does little good, after the fact, simply to say that something did or did not work. Because many of the programs must be there anyway, it is much more important to ask How does the program work? How can we make it work better? Which kind of treatment works better for which kind of client? How can treatment be improved to improve client outcomes? If the program must be there anyway, study it longitudinally and ensure rigor through replication, that is, testing the treatment theory, retesting, refining, and so on.

Before testing the pure science question, "Which program works better?" it is reasonable to develop stronger theoretical models of how the program works and learn to measure and improve its key components. In studies of drug and fertilizer treatments, we measure and manipulate our chemicals. Likewise, before doing social experiments, we should know how to measure and manipulate our social treatments. Effectiveness cannot be expected without successful program implementation. To improve our programs does not require experiments, but it does require fairly good measurement and reasonably good replicability of utoS.

Construct Validity of the Observation. As is the case with the treatment, the observation of the effect is only one representative of the class of possible observations that measure the particular construct of interest. The methods of observation used to measure a construct can vary as much as the units and the treatments. For example, there can be many and varied paper and pencil measures in terms of format, content, validity, and reliability; the persons administering the measurement vary; the characteristics of observers vary; the format of observing operations varies from in-person interviews to telephone interviews to group interviews to mail questionnaires to unobtrusive measures; and the occasion and setting of observations vary.

Mono-Method Bias. Mono-method bias refers to the method we use to measure the operationalizations. When all measures use the same method of recording, there is risk of mono-method bias. In other words, the effect depends to some extent on the way we measure it. For example, level of stress within an individual may be somewhat different when measured using different methods such as a self-report questionnaire, physiological measures (blood pressure, muscle tension), or an observer's recording of the amount of job stress behavior exhibited by an employee. Using only one measure of stress may bias the observation toward one type of stress with a resulting inaccurate estimate of stress in general.

Interaction of Observation with Unit, Treatment, and Setting. Aspects of treatments can affect observations. For example, in our substance abuse project, we were concerned that, even though subjects had improved, the observations obtained at discharge might reflect their trepidation, anger, or disappointment at being discharged, especially if the discharge was because of a relapse. In this case, anger at discharge could distort the observation of the program effect. Also, subjects can be sensitive to being in an enhanced treatment group and report that they are doing better than they are in order to please the researchers (Johnston and Swift, this volume). Additionally, the setting can interact with the observation. For example, focus group research has found that subjects respond more freely when they feel that they are talking with people who are like them (Krueger, 1988). Different people respond better to different types of observation methods, and certain methods are appropriate for certain types of people in certain situations.

Observation of Treatment. The observations of treatment in experiments have traditionally been straightforward; for example, the drug was administered or not; the electric shock was delivered at the right place, intensity, and duration; the fertilizer was applied in the proper amount. However, the observation of the implementation of a complex health and social service such as community care for homeless substance abusers over a year's time is not nearly so straightforward. Our ability to validly measure the kind, quality, quantity, and appropriateness of complex treatments (and controls) is in its early stages of development, but it is essential to the evaluation of complex social programs (Conrad and Roberts-Gray, 1988). Multiple methods of observation are recommended to assess the success of treatment implementation (Lam, Hartwell, and Jekel, this volume; Johnston and Swift, this volume) and the interpretability of results. Multiple methods can also help to reduce inappropriate certainty of conclusions (Mark and Shotland, 1987).

Reactions to Experimental Observations. Reactions to experimentation may also affect observations, whether the observation is of the cause (the treatment) or the effect. In the competitive experimental versus control environment, data collectors may selectively choose records that support a study hypothesis. In providing data on a study outcome, an agency may, in its effort to look good, provide data to the investigators that will support or refute the study hypotheses. On controversial issues, agency staff have lost or falsified documents or results that would reflect poorly on them. It is often the case that both experimental and control staff have negative reactions to the demands of observation. They may be perceived as too much paperwork and too much time when clinical demands are already excessive (Devine, Wright, and Joyner, this volume; McAuliffe and Ashery, 1993). This reaction may be intensified for control providers who may be less motivated because they resent the fact that their clients are not getting the innovative treatment. This tendency may also be intensified when a rival experimental treatment is seen as a threat.

Construct Validity of the Setting. The setting (S) is the social, political, economic, and geographical context of the study. The setting in which a program occurs may vary greatly. A smoking cessation program's effect in a box manufacturing company in Chicago, Illinois will not necessarily be the same as the effects of similar programs in Birmingham, Seattle, Mexico City, Beijing, Paris, or Cairo. Additionally, settings vary over time. The election of a new chief executive officer, governor, or president can have a profound effect on the setting, which, in turn, can influence the program's effectiveness, for better or worse. The implication for more generalizable research is that it is necessary to understand the populations of UTOS and *UTOS to which we wish to generalize before we conduct experiments. This can be accomplished with representative sampling of populations followed by classification of subpopulations (for example, see Conrad, Hughes, Hanrahan, and Wang, 1993; Conrad and

Buelow, 1990). Typically, in experiments the setting is described but not compared with other settings. Without valid measures of various settings, generalizing from one setting to another is problematic.

Reactions to the Experiment. As we noted earlier, the setting can mute or intensify effects depending on interactions with units, treatments, and observations (Roberts-Gray and Scheirer, 1988). Just as subjects react to experimentation, the setting can be reactive. Ashery and McAuliffe (1992) noted that local programs will often be reluctant to trust their clients to a new program, whether randomized or not, until they learn the program's services, policies, staff, and eligibility criteria. Local agencies may distrust researchers based on prior dealings (Wright, Devine, and Eddington, 1993; Lam, Hartwell, and Jekel, this volume) and may view the research demonstration project as a competitor. Some will disagree with or misunderstand the innovation. Others will object to randomization because they think their clients are being used as guinea pigs. Others object that some of those who are best suited for the innovation are turned away because they lost the coin flip (Lam, Hartwell, and Jekel, this volume). For these reasons, local programs may steer clients away, with the result that the unit construct is distorted. Developing a new program may require many meetings with referral agencies to familiarize them with the new program, its goals, and the criteria defining the target population (Stevens and others, 1993). Finally, an unpleasant experience with randomization can leave the community angry and resentful toward the university and toward research as a field (Lam, Hartwell, and Jekel, this volume; Johnston and Swift, this volume).

Construct Validity over Time. The question, "To which periods in the past and the future does the observed causal relationship pertain?" is a crucial one. The randomized experiment was designed to address the timeless pure science issue, "Does the treatment work?" Therefore, it may not account for the fact that social programs change, adapting to changing times and environments. As Cronbach (1982) has noted, society needs answers to important social issues and, in many cases, timeliness is crucial. This is because, unlike more stable agricultural or biomedical issues, social issues tend to arise unexpectedly and may come and go. For example, the recent dramatic increases in homelessness, drug abuse, and violent crime have arisen suddenly and unexpectedly. Society cannot wait for experiments to be conducted before designing programs to address these problems. An experiment may take two years to design, approve, and fund, three years to implement, a year to analyze, and another year to publish. This is a seven-year information lag. In that time, the problems may have changed, the ideas about methods of addressing them may have changed, funding may have gone up or down, and the settings and populations where the major problems occur may be different. Therefore, in addition to the unacceptable time period, the findings may be obsolete when they are published. Again, this problem can be addressed with longitudinal, theory-driven studies that focus on the construct validity of utoS.

Improving Future Evaluations

A key to improving future evaluations is improving evaluators' knowledge of evaluation options. The experimental paradigm is well-established and its logic is compelling. Shadish and Epstein (1987) found that the Campbell and Stanley (1963) monograph has had by far the greatest impact on evaluators, whereas the impact of other major evaluation theorists appeared relatively small. If our evaluation repertoire is limited or we believe that the experiment is superior, this may limit our choice of research methods. Shadish and Epstein also found that 75 percent of the evaluators studied did not recognize Cronbach's UTOS model. If nothing else, this chapter should use UTOS to raise healthy questions and doubts about the adequacy of the current state-of-the-art experimental paradigm to answer questions in social and health services research. As the studies referred to here indicate, randomized experiments are extremely difficult to implement properly in field settings. A great deal of preparation is needed before a successful experiment can be done. In the field of evaluation, studies like those reported in this book are unusual (Heckman, 1992), but they are needed to examine the impact of threats to validity on experimental results. Without such studies, we may tend to underestimate the impact of these threats.

Stages of Research Development. Rather than insisting immediately on answering causal questions, it is probably more useful and appropriate to establish the existence of relationships and their signs (Cook, 1993). With good replicability, the strength and directionality of cause can become clearer as time goes on. To do so, we need treatment and setting measures that are valid and reliable. We can measure samples of treatments (Conrad and Buelow, 1990; Conrad, Hughes, Hanrahan, and Wang, 1993) and settings, use these samples to classify the phenomena, and use the measures to develop and test theories of how subclasses work. In this way, we will be clarifying the construct validity and generalizability of our studies.

Observational, developmental improvement studies are needed to specify the nature of the program, its proper implementation (program manual), and the measurement of its key components. In studying samples of projects, logic models (theories) should be developed that explain how the treatments work to influence outcomes (Wholey, 1979). Stakeholders should be involved in the development of the logic models through focus groups, expert panels, and as coinvestigators. Rather than the scientist in the lab transferred into the field, the research model should involve a researcher as a builder of coalitions that work to build consensus (read "theory") about how programs work. Measurement models should be developed to test the validity of the logic models that result. The validity of the measures should be ascertained. The measures can then be used to test the logic models and to promote program improvement. The development of measures that clinicians can use for quality improvement is important for the conduct of theory-driven empirical studies. Studies designed to promote continuous improvement over a considerable time period will be more likely to involve providers and other stakeholders to ensure the usefulness of measures and procedures. Clinical usefulness will ensure greater clinical acceptance of and support for research.

To prepare for experiments to test clear, crucial, causal questions, time series designs can be used that develop and test program theories; improve the program, then retest, and so on. With the understanding of the program and the development of the measures, it will be possible to conduct multisite experiments to test causal hypotheses when these are appropriate.

What does this mean for the future? Packages of studies are needed (Berk and others, 1985) that include the foregoing components. Teams from multiple sites, employing investigators from several disciplines and using multiple methods, will be necessary. These studies will require a degree of cooperation that is unusual today; however, we believe they can be achieved in the near future. As noted elsewhere (Conrad, Hultman, and Lyons, 1993), the NIAAA cooperative agreement (Orwin, Cordray, and Huebner, this volume) employed multiple methods, multiple sites, and the involvement of researchers and clinicians as coprincipal investigators. The open, critical dialogue from the NIAAA project fostered the frank revelation of practical difficulties with experiments that made this volume possible. It is a good foundation on which to build.

References

Argyris, C. *Inner Contradictions of Rigorous Research*. New York: Academic Press, 1980.

Ashery, R. S., and McAuliffe, W. E. "Implementation Issues and Techniques in Randomized Trials of Outpatient Psychosocial Treatments for Drug Abusers: Recruitment of Subjects." *American Journal of Drug and Alcohol Abuse*, 1992, *18* (3), 305–329.

Berk, R. A., and others. "Social Policy Experimentation: A Position Paper." *Evaluation Review*, 1985, *9* (4), 387–429.

Berk, R. A., Smyth, G. K., and Sherman, L. W. "When Random Assignment Fails: Some Lessons from the Minneapolis Spouse Abuse Experiment." *Journal of Quantitative Criminology*, 1988, *4* (3), 209–223.

Bloom, H. S. "Accounting for No-Shows in Experimental Evaluation Designs." *Evaluation Review*, 1984, *8* (2), 225–246.

Boruch, R. F., and Wothke, W. "Seven Kinds of Randomization Plans for Designing Field Experiments." In R. F. Boruch and W. Wothke (eds.), *Randomization and Field Experimentation*. New Directions for Program Evaluation, no. 28. San Francisco: Jossey-Bass, 1985.

Brekke, J. S. "What Do We Really Know about Community Support Programs?: Strategies for Better Monitoring." *Hospital and Community Psychiatry*, 1988, *39*, 946–952.

Campbell, D. T. "Methods for the Experimenting Society." *Evaluation Practice*, 1991, *12* (3), 223–260.

Campbell, D. T., and Stanley, J. C. *Experimental and Quasi-Experimental Designs for Research*. Chicago: Rand McNally, 1963.

Chen, H., and Rossi, P. "Evaluating with Sense: The Theory-Driven Approach." *Evaluation Review*, 1983, *7*, 283-302.

Chubin, D. E., and Hackett, E. J. *Peerless Science: Peer Review and U.S. Science Policy*. Albany: State University of New York Press, 1990.

Conrad, K. J., and Buelow, J. R. "Developing and Testing Program Classification and Function Theories." In L. Bickman (ed.), *Advances in Program Theory*. New Directions for Program Evaluation, no. 47. San Francisco: Jossey-Bass, 1990.

Conrad, K. J., Hughes, S. L., Hanrahan, P., and Wang, S. "Classification of Adult Day Care: A Cluster Analysis of Services and Activities." *Journal of Gerontology: Social Sciences*, 1993, *48* (3), S112–122.

Conrad, K. J., Hultman, C. I., and Lyons, J. S. "Treatment of the Chemically Dependent Homeless: Theory and Implementation in Fourteen American Projects." *Alcoholism Treatment Quarterly*, 1993, *10* (3–4).

Conrad, K. J., and Miller, T. Q. "Measuring and Testing Program Philosophy." In L. Bickman (ed.), *Using Program Theory in Evaluation*. New Directions for Program Evaluation, no. 33. San Francisco: Jossey-Bass, 1987.

Conrad, K. J., and Roberts-Gray, C. (eds.). *Evaluating Program Environments*. New Directions for Program Evaluation, no. 40. San Francisco: Jossey-Bass, 1988.

Conrad, K. M., Conrad, K. J., and Walcott-McQuigg, J. "Threats To Internal Validity In Worksite Health Promotion Program Research: Common Problems and Possible Solutions." *American Journal of Health Promotion*, 1991, *6*, 112–122.

Cook, T. D. "A Quasi-Sampling Theory of the Generalization of Causal Relationships." In L. B. Sechrest and A. G. Scott (eds.), *Understanding Causes and Generalizing About Them*. New Directions for Program Evaluation, no. 57. San Francisco: Jossey-Bass, 1993.

Cook, T. D., and Campbell, D. T. *Quasi-Experimentation: Design and Analysis Issues for Field Settings*. Chicago: Rand McNally, 1979.

Cronbach, L. J. *Designing Evaluations of Educational and Social Programs*. San Francisco: Jossey-Bass, 1982.

Goldstein, H. *Multilevel Models in Educational and Social Research*. New York: Oxford University Press, 1987.

Heckman, J. J. "Randomization and Social Policy Experimentation." In C. F. Manski and I. Garfinkel (eds.), *Evaluating Welfare and Training Programs*. Cambridge, Mass.: Harvard University Press, 1992, pp. 201–230.

Hennessy, C., and Hennessy, M. "Community-Based Long-Term Care for the Elderly: Evaluation Practice Reconsidered." *Medical Care Review*, 1990, *47*, 221–259.

Howard, K. I., Cox, W. M., and Saunders, S. M. "Attrition in Substance Abuse Comparative Treatment Research: The Illusion of Randomization." National Institute on Drug Abuse Review on Psychotherapy and Counseling in the Treatment of Drug Abuse, Rockville, Md., May 18–19, 1989.

Kaluzny, A. (ed.). *Cancer Control in the Rubber Industry*. Final report. Chapel Hill: School of Public Health: Lineberger Cancer Research Center, University of North Carolina, 1987.

Koepke, S., and Flay, B. "Levels of Analysis." In M. T. Braverman (ed.), *Evaluating Health Promotion Programs*. New Directions for Program Evaluation, no. 43. San Francisco: Jossey-Bass, 1989.

Krueger, R. A. *Focus Groups: A Practical Guide for Applied Research*. Newbury Park, Calif.: Sage, 1988.

Levitan, S. A. *Evaluation of Federal Social Programs: An Uncertain Impact*. Center for Social Policy Studies, The George Washington University, Washington, D.C., 1992.

McAuliffe, W. E., and Ashery, R. S. "Implementation Issues and Techniques in Randomized Trials of Outpatient Psychosocial Treatments for Drug Abusers. II. Clinical and Administrative Issues." *American Journal of Drug and Alcohol Abuse*, 1993, *19* (1), 35–50.

Mark, M. M., and Shotland, R. L. *Multiple Methods in Program Evaluation*. New Directions for Program Evaluation, no. 35. San Francisco: Jossey-Bass, 1987.

Messick, S. "Validity." In R. Linn (ed.), *Educational Measurement*. New York: Macmillan, 1989.

Prochaska, J. O., DiClemente, C. C., and Norcross, J. C. "In Search of How People Change: Applications to Addictive Behaviors." *American Psychologist*, 1992, *47* (9), 1102–1114.

Roberts-Gray, C., and Scheirer, M. A. "Checking the Congruence Between a Program and Its Organizational Environment." In K. J. Conrad (ed.), *Evaluating Program Environments*. New Directions for Program Evaluation, no. 40. San Francisco: Jossey-Bass, 1988.

Shadish, W. R., and Epstein, R. "Patterns of Program Evaluation Practice among Members of the Evaluation Research Society and Evaluation Network." *Evaluation Review*, 1987, *11* (3), 555–590.

Stevens, S. J., and others. "A Therapeutic Community Model for Treatment of Homeless Alcohol and Drug Users in Tucson, Arizona." *Alcoholism Treatment Quarterly*, 1993, *10* (3/4), 21–33.

Wheat, J. R., and others. "Does Workplace Health Promotion Decrease Medical Claims?" *American Journal of Preventive Medicine*, 1992, *8*, 110–114.

White, R. N., and Weidman, J. C. "Doing Evaluation Research for Public Agencies: Problems with Random Assignment of Clients." *Sociological Practice*, 1983, *4* (2), 185–215.

Whiting-O'Keefe, Q. E., Henke, C., and Simborg, D. W. "Choosing the Correct Unit of Analysis in Medical Care Experiments." *Medical Care*, 1984, *22*, 1101–1114.

Widman, H., Wolfe, D., and Manning, M. *Health Builder: An Evaluation Study of a Comprehensive Health Promotion Program*. Final report submitted to W. K. Kellogg Foundation. Blue Cross and Blue Shield of Northern Ohio, 1987.

Wholey, J. S. *Evaluation: Promise and Performance*. Washington, D.C.: Urban Institute, 1979.

Wright, J. D., Devine, J. A., and Eddington, N. "The New Orleans Homeless Substance Abusers Project." In K. J. Conrad, C. I. Hultman, J. S. Lyons (eds.), *The Treatment of Chemically Dependent Homeless: Theory and Implementation in Fourteen American Projects. Alcoholism Treatment Quarterly*, 1993, *10* (3–4).

KENDON J. CONRAD *is associate director of the Midwest Center for Health Services and Policy Research at Hines VA Hospital. He is also associate professor at the University of Illinois at Chicago, School of Public Health, where he is associate director of the Center for Health Services Research.*

KAREN M. CONRAD *is assistant professor of public health nursing and director of the Occupational Health Nursing Program in the College of Nursing at the University of Illinois at Chicago.*

Because of the differential perspectives, needs, and interests that undergird clinical and research objectives, program staff may wittingly or unwittingly sabotage randomization. A case study of the New Orleans Homeless Substance Abusers Program amply documents this process.

Issues in Implementing a Randomized Experiment in a Field Setting

Joel A. Devine, James D. Wright, Laurie M. Joyner

The rationale for randomized experiments is a strong one; no other research design is better suited to ruling out competing explanations for the observed effects. In actual practice, however, randomization proves to be very much like chastity: an ideal toward which one may strive, not an absolute standard that one actually expects to achieve. It is useful to note the parallel between randomization in experiments and random sampling in surveys. Even well-designed and well-executed surveys will have some nonresponse (and thus, self-selection into and out of the sample). Because people who choose not to participate do so for some reason, every probability sample ends up containing nonprobabilistic components. So too with randomization in field-experimental settings: However tightly researchers attempt to control placement of subjects in experimental and control conditions, some "leakage" inevitably occurs. The task in survey research is to keep nonresponse to a minimum; the task in field experiments is to keep "leakage" to a minimum. Still, because leakage does occur, elaborate statistical controls are often necessary to account for any initial nonequivalence introduced by the failure to randomize, just as would be the case with a non-experimental design.In theory, analysis of an experimental outcome requires little more than the calculation of two means and a test for the significance of their difference; in fact, analysis of experimental data on human subjects can become as "messy" as the analysis of cross-sectional data.

New Orleans Homeless Substance Abusers Program (NOHSAP)

NOHSAP was a residentially based demonstration project targeted to homeless substance abusers in the New Orleans area. Among large cities, New Orleans ranks second in its overall poverty rate; poverty in the city is heavily concentrated within the 65 percent black majority. Estimates of the size of the city's one-night homeless population vary from 3,000 to 12,000 (Rudegeair, 1990), of whom about 80 percent are African-Americans and about 25 percent are women. As one of the nation's poorest cities, New Orleans offers very little in the area of social and human services, least of all to the homeless.

Treatment Goals and Intervention Philosophy. NOHSAP was designed to achieve four principal goals: a substance-free existence (permanent sobriety), residential stability (permanent housing of more than minimal adequacy), economic independence (jobs and incomes adequate to sustain an independent existence), and a reduction in family estrangement. The philosophy behind the NOHSAP intervention was that one cannot begin to address the alcohol and drug problems of homeless substance abusers until they are first stabilized residentially, that is, until they are provided with a clean and secure place to live where sobriety is a positively valued norm.

The essence of the clinical intervention was to provide the proper unlearning and learning (resocialization) environment and to create a social and physical context that rewards and encourages these changes.

Intervention Model. NOHSAP was designed as a three-phase intervention: social detoxification, transitional care, and extended care/independent living. Detoxification was a seven-day program of sobering up, introduction to Alcoholics Anonymous and Narcotics Anonymous principles, twice-daily group meetings, some counseling, and limited assessment and case management. In theory, clients were to be assessed by clinical staff at the end of the seven-day period as to their motivation and suitability for further treatment. Clients judged not motivated or not suitable were discharged and released to the streets. Clients deemed suitable for further treatment theoretically went into a pool of eligibles from which they were either randomized into treatment or released back to the streets.

Transitional care (TC) consisted of a twenty-one-day program involving more extensive assessment and case management, twice-daily group meetings, placement in an off-campus alcohol or drug group, and general reinforcement of any positive steps taken during detoxification. Getting people to stop using drugs and alcohol proved to be the easy part of treatment; the hard part was teaching clients how to deal with their sobriety. Much of the counseling in TC focused on managing stress without alcohol or drugs.

Clients successfully completing TC became eligible for the extended care/independent living (ECIL) program, a twelve-month program that continued the interventions and strategies begun during TC while also providing

General Equivalency Diploma services, job training, and job placement. Movement from TC to ECIL was determined by the same randomization process governing earlier entry into TC: Clinical staff determined client suitability for further treatment. From this pool of eligibles, clients were either randomized into ECIL or released.

Client Characteristics. NOHSAP saw its first clients in February 1991. Over the next fourteen months, 670 clients were baselined into the study; 505 (75.4 percent) became "controls" (meaning that they received seven days of detoxification and were then released back to the community) and 165 (24.6 percent) became "treatments" (meaning that they were offered TC or TC + ECIL). Clients were overwhelmingly African-American (82.2 percent), relatively young (mean age of 34), and predominantly male (75 percent). Most had some work history and a few job skills, but as a whole were ill-prepared for employment in the postindustrial economy. A slight majority (52.5 percent) were polysubstance abusive; about half (47.6 percent) had alcohol problems; most (84.9 percent) were crack addicts; small proportions abused heroin and other illicit drugs. A quarter (26.9 percent) of the respondents had previous treatment for their alcohol problems, and more than half (54.0 percent) had prior treatment for their other drug problems. Thus, in the main, ours was a sample of multiply troubled, young, black, crack-addicted homeless males. They could be considered representative of what has come to be called the urban underclass (Devine and Wright, 1993). (Additional details on characteristics of the sample and on program design and participation are given in Wright and Devine, 1993a, 1993b; Wright, Devine, and Eddington, 1993).

Randomization in Theory: The NOHSAP Design

At NOHSAP's outset, the first 24 clients deemed eligible and appropriate by the clinical staff were to be placed in TC. Subsequent placements were to be made via randomization out of a pool of detoxed clients whom the clinical staff deemed eligible and appropriate for further placement. Placement in ECIL was to be accomplished in the same manner, with the added proviso that only clients successfully completing TC would be eligible.

Once randomized selection kicked in, we hoped to maintain an inclusion probability of .5 (for each available treatment slot, there would be two eligible clients). Based on program experience with a preexisting social detoxification facility, we also had reason to believe that the aggregate ratio of eligibles to openings would often exceed the 2:1 standard—even allowing for probable administrative "oversell." We also recognized that program-specific and demographically dictated inclusion probabilities would have to be stratified and necessarily would vary on a day-to-day basis because placement depended on space availability and the fact that male, female, and family clients required separate housing.

Hypothetically, a less satisfactory alternative existed, namely, to let the research goal of stable and equal inclusion probabilities dictate service delivery.

In all likelihood, this alternative would have involved discharging eligible clients back to the streets for possible later entry into the program. In addition to treatment interruption (and the associated risks of undermining individual treatment success as well as introducing possible contamination and bias), this method would have required us to underuse treatment capacity. Treatment slots would have had to be kept empty to realize a smooth client flow and stable and equal inclusion probabilities. Even this method would not really ensure the desired outcome because individuals could (and would) decide to leave when they wanted to—often against clinical advice. Moreover, even assuming that the desired research goal of stable and equal inclusion probabilities could be met, such an outcome would necessitate the squandering of scarce resources in a community already lacking critical treatment slots: We were not about to let the randomization tail wag the treatment dog.

Within these constraints, then, the design established a three-step process for selection into the two treatment phases: (1) as treatment slots opened, program staff would develop lists of eligibles (thus, within each treatment phase, multiple lists might be generated—for example, one for single males, another for single females, still another for females with children—all depending upon actual space availability); (2) after actual randomization, the co-principal investigators would then communicate the assignments back to the clinical site; and (3) program staff would implement the program, informing clients of the results (an obviously difficult task in the negative case) and finalize discharge or further treatment planning.

This division of labor was established by mutual agreement between the clinical and research teams before program commencement. This arrangement clearly reflected the predominance of a critical research objective and because the selection mechanism wrested some programmatic control from the clinical staff, it was recognized as a potential source of conflict between the program and research staffs. However, the apparent loss of control appeared to be mitigated by the fact that the clinical staff was charged with determining the criteria for eligibility and thus was given total discretion over the placement of individuals on the selection lists.

Based on our previous experience and a large literature on the point, we anticipated that there would be considerable staff resistance to the idea of randomizing clients into and out of treatment. We therefore made it absolutely clear from the beginning that the judgement concerning further treatment was *strictly* and *entirely* a clinical decision and that the research team was neither inclined nor qualified to second-guess these decisions. We felt—wrongly, as it turned out—that the treatment staff would be more accepting of the idea of randomizing from a pool of eligibles if they had complete control over which clients went into the pool. This also had the convenient effect of "matching" randomized treatments and controls on motivation and suitability for further treatment.

At the same time, this arrangement was thought to provide some emotional benefit or cover to the program staff in that it would absolve clinicians from the responsibility for placement decisions. In a situation where resources were scarce, randomization would solve the ethical and emotional dilemmas of denying services to some who were in need. Randomization promised equitable treatment, no favoritism, no special privilege, and it afforded an important rationalization: "I (or we) didn't deny you treatment, the researchers did." Moreover, if program effects were modest, as they always are, blame could be assigned to the randomization. ("They put the wrong people in treatment.")

Although this selection process necessarily delimited clinicians' absolute control over placement, it did provide the program staff with critical and defining input. They would determine the pool of eligibles. With some cleverness, they could control the outcome. It was also recognized that this arrangement afforded the clinical staff the opportunity to "cream" clients by placing the names of only those clients whom they considered sufficiently motivated or potentially likely to succeed on the lists. Given the documented ineffectiveness of most alcohol and drug treatment programs, however, we did not consider any likely "creaming" to be a problem but rather an asset; effective "creaming" would prevent squandering scarce treatment resources on unsuitable clients. As researchers, we took the attitude that rather than jeopardizing the validity of the study, these decisions represented necessary clinical judgements. Our task was to model it.

Moving Toward Implementation: Putting Randomization into Practice

Before start-up, a series of meetings were held between the research and clinical staffs to work out project-related issues and to develop interstaff familiarity and rapport. Going into the project, we assumed that there would be the usual difficulties resulting from the different goals, sensitivities, and backgrounds of the research and program teams. As expected, a number of the clinical staff expressed reservations concerning randomization as a selection mechanism, the research team's desire to establish explicit eligibility criteria (be they objective or subjective), the perception that the research staff was going to second-guess and judge the program staff (and perhaps, expose them to embarrassment or other sanctions), the seemingly obsessive demands of the researchers for documentation, and so on. The generic undercurrent was, of course, an oft-sung refrain: the intrusion (real or apparent) of the researchers into the program domain and the perception that the research agenda, goals, and culture would come to dominate the initiative.

Sensitive to these concerns, the research team adopted a hands-off approach to all clinical matters. Our position was that it was the clinical side's job to do good; the research job was merely to document the good that was being done. Still, many treatment staff seemed permanently anxious that their work was being graded by the evaluation team.

Such perceptions on the part of the program staff were neither surprising nor altogether unfounded. The literature is, of course, replete with well-documented inter- and intraorganizational strains between program and research goals and staffs (see, for instance, Rodman and Kolodny, 1977; Sonnichsen, 1989; Weiss, 1977). The heart of the program–research conflict is that researchers are interested in knowing whether a program worked whereas program people are interested in showing that the program worked; in that subtle distinction lies a world of pain (see Rossi and Freeman, 1989; chapters 3 and 9 discuss goal conflicts in evaluation).

Despite a shared (at least in part) objective and the widespread development of positive and collegial relations among members of the two teams, only a Dr. Pangloss could ignore the disparate backgrounds of the program and research people and their distinct organizational cultures. Moreover, the sheer magnitude of the task at hand, and the fact that the clinical subcontractor would be tripling its size in only a few months, suggested that some difficulties would lie ahead.

At the same time, it is important not to overstate this situation. A positive working foundation was achieved; relations were cordial, commitment and cooperation were high, communication seemed open, and channels for resolving anticipated conflicts had been established. Finally, procedures for delivering services, gaining data, and selecting clients for treatment had seemingly been sorted out.

Concerning randomization specifically, the following questions and concerns were articulated by various members of the program staff at various times:

Why is randomization necessary (or, in its declarative form, Randomization is not necessary so why do we have to do it that way)?
What is randomization (or, why are we choosing treatment clients haphazardly)?
Randomization wrests control of services away from us, the program people, the ones on the front lines, the ones who know what's going on.
Randomization seems inefficient (why deny treatment to a "worthy" client and provide it to an "unworthy" one?).
I can't tell you why I think someone should be eligible, it's just a gut reaction.
Randomization seems heartless and unethical.

These concerns constituted a series of potential barriers to the effective implementation of randomization in a field setting. However, we did not consider these particularly problematic—we fully expected some sensitivity regarding such matters and would have been surprised had it not surfaced. We sought to disabuse the staff of the notion that their decisions regarding eligibility necessarily implied success or even a high probability of success. After all, if one could make highly effective determinations of who would succeed in treatment, studies of this sort would be unnecessary. We reiterated our

position that the determination of eligibility was a clinical decision and necessarily an imperfect one. Our only concern was to find out how this decision
was made, the criteria used, and how critical concerns such as motivation
were assessed.

Randomization in Practice: The NOHSAP Experience

Turning now to an examination of randomization as it was actually implemented, it is clear that these potential barriers were firmly realized. Data on
the actual randomization of clients into the two treatment groups are summarized in Table 2.1. As indicated, only a third (32.1 percent) of the 165 clients
entering TC and a fourth (24.6 percent) of the 57 clients going into ECIL were
actually randomized into treatment. If we exclude the first 24 (14.5 percent)
and 20 (35.1 percent) clients in TC and ECIL respectively, as per the research
plan described above, the figures improve, but only marginally. Even then, less
than two-fifths of the TC (37.6 percent) and ECIL (37.8 percent) populations
were randomly assigned.

As the data in Table 2.1 further indicate, 8 (or 4.8 percent) and 5 (8.8 percent) of the clients entering TC and ECIL respectively were actually randomized out of treatment only to enter it when other clients who had been
randomized in chose to not enter the treatment programs. The latter, that is,
clients randomized in but not opting for treatment, numbered 11 (6.7 percent
of the actually enrolled TC group) and 9 (15.8 percent of ECIL).

Thus, even allowing that randomization would not commence until full
treatment capacity had been achieved, one cannot escape the fact that almost
half (48.5 percent) of the persons receiving TC treatment and almost a third
(31.6 percent) of those gaining access to ECIL were selected in a manner
inconsistent with the experimental design. This should most certainly raise
questions about the equivalence of the two groups and the experimental efficacy of NOHSAP.

Table 2.2 reports evidence on this critical issue of equivalence in terms of
randomization status and treatment status. These data consist of composite
scores from the Addiction Severity Index (ASI—see Fureman, Parikh, Bragg,
and McLellan, 1990), a part of the baseline interview administered to all
clients on their second or third day in detox. The ASI composites provide convenient summaries of the degree of client problems in seven areas of life functioning. Concerning randomization status (Panel A), the data reveal no
significant differences between clients who were randomized and those who
were not; that is, the two groups are not statistically distinguishable. Thus,
whether a client's placement in NOHSAP was determined by the outcome of
randomization or by some other nonrandom selection factor is itself a random variable with respect to the ASI composite scores, an obviously encouraging result.

Panel B reports data for the comparison of all treatments against all controls regardless of whether clients were randomized. Initially, these results are

Table 2.1. Randomization Status and Inclusion Probabilities

	Treatment Condition	
	Level I Transitional Care (165)	Level II ECIL (57)
Number of Treatment Clients (N)		
Number of clients randomized in and entering program	53	14
Number randomized in with inclusion probability < 1.00[a]	27	10
Number randomized in with inclusion probability = 1.00[b]	26	4
Number of clients randomized out but still entering program[c]	8	5
Number of clients randomized in but *not* entering program	11	9
Number of initial clients entering before start of randomization	24	20
Number of other entering clients not randomized	80	18
Percentage of clients randomized in and entering program	32.1 / 37.6[d]	24.6 / 37.8[d]
Percentage randomized in with inclusion probability < 1.00[a]	16.4 / 19.1[d]	17.5 / 27.0[d]
Percentage randomized in with inclusion probability - 1.00[b]	15.8 / 18.4[d]	7.0 / 10.8[d]
Percentage of clients randomized out but still entering program[c]	4.8 / 5.7[d]	8.8 / 13.5[d]
Percentage of clients randomized in but *not* entering program	6.7[e] / 7.8[f]	15.8[e] / 24.3[f]
Percentage of initial clients entering before start of randomization	14.5 / —	35.1 / —
Percentage of other entering clients not randomized	48.5 / 56.7[d]	31.6 / 48.6[d]

[a] Number of eligible clients exceeds number of spaces available.
[b] Number of available spaces exceeds number of eligible clients.
[c] Previously unanticipated space becomes available.
[d] Percent excluding initial clients entering before randomization.
[e] Percent of enrolled N.
[f] Percent of enrolled excluding intitial clients entering before randomization.

Table 2.2. Equivalence Between Groups, Baseline Data, and Tests of Difference on ASI Composite Scores[a]

Panel A: Randomization Status[b]

ASI Composite[c]	Randomized clients		Nonrandomized clients		Pooled variance t-test	
	Mean	S.D.	Mean	S.D.	t Value	2-Tail Prob.
Medical status	.225	.321	.233	.339	.21	.836
Employment status	.783	.233	.810	.213	1.15	.251
Alcohol use	.298	.304	.305	.315	.22	.823
Drug use	.229	.111	.231	.128	.15	.881
Legal status	.149	.229	.166	.241	.72	.471
Family/social status	.246	.252	.277	.268	1.06	.291
Psychiatric status	.407	.180	.413	.213	.26	.793

Panel B: Treatment Status[d]

ASI Composite[c]	Treatment Group		Control Group		Pooled variance t-test	
	Mean	S.D.	Mean	S.D.	t-Value	2-Tail Prob.
Medical status	.255	.338	.224	.335	−1.05	.294
Employment status	.844	.202	.793	.219	−2.62	.009**
Alcohol use	.247	.286	.323	.320	2.68	.007**
Drug use	.231	.120	.231	.127	−.05	.959
Legal status	.164	.213	.163	.218	−.04	.970
Family/social status	.279	.267	.270	.266	−.37	.713
Psychiatric status	.418	.189	.410	.214	−.41	.681

[a] See Fureman, Parikh, Bragg, and McLellan, 1990.
[b] Randomized (in/out of treatment; $N = 105$) vs. nonrandomized clients ($N = 565$)
[c] Higher scores indicate greater problem severity.
** Significant difference ($p \leq .01$).

less encouraging in that two significant differences are observed: (1) treatment clients had significantly more severe employment problems than control clients (on average, treatment clients worked one-and-a-half fewer days and earned seventy-five fewer dollars in the month prior to treatment); and (2) control clients had significantly more severe alcohol problems than treatment clients (controls reported more days drinking to intoxication, were spending more money per month on alcohol, and were more troubled by their alcohol problems). Given the program goals, these differences are of considerable concern, although it is comforting that no significant differences are observed on the other variables.

Further analysis of the data reveals a straightforward demographic explanation of the observed nonequivalence. In brief, women were much more likely to be placed in TC and ECIL than men were. Among the 505 men who were baselined, 86 percent ended up in the control group and only 14 percent were placed in further treatment; among the 165 women who were baselined, 53 percent went into the control group and 47 percent were placed in treatment. Thus, women were more than three times as likely as men to be selected for treatment. (Among women with children, the bias was even stronger.) Calculating in the other direction, 83 percent of the control clients were men, whereas men comprise only 47 percent of the TC treatments and 51 percent of the ECIL treatments. The zero-order comparison between treatments and controls in Panel B therefore compares one group that is dominated by males with a second group where males and females are represented in roughly equal numbers.

In analysis reported elsewhere (see Wright and Devine, 1993b), we document significant male–female differences at baseline on a number of factors, including alcohol use (men were more likely than women to have alcohol problems) and employment (in general, the women had more troubled work histories than the men), exactly the pattern shown in the zero-order treatment-control comparisons. This suggests that the observed nonequivalence between treatments and controls may be attributable to a gender-based selection bias.

To address this issue, we stepwise-regressed the seven ASI composite scores on gender and treatment status, with gender entered first (analysis not presented, see Wright and Devine, 1993b, Table 20). Gender is a significant predictor of every ASI composite; however, when gender is held constant, treatment status is not significantly related to any ASI composite score. Critically, the significant zero-order differences in alcohol and employment problems disappear once gender is controlled. Thus, the failure to randomize resulted in a gross overrepresentation of women among the treatments, but once this factor is taken into account, the initial nonequivalence between treatment and control groups vanishes.

One can only speculate on the reasons why women, especially women with children, were much more likely than men to end up in the treatment groups. Perhaps women were generally more compliant with the treatment ethos and therefore more likely to be selected. There may also have been some belief among clinical staff that the women were better bets for treatment. We suspect, however, that the answer is much less complicated. For nearly all NOHSAP clients, failure to be selected for TC or ECIL meant a return to life in the streets, a fact of which clinical staff were certainly aware. Given the choice between condemning a man or a woman to such an existence, most people would find it less troubling to condemn the man, and most certainly so if the woman also had dependent children in her care. The sentiment is no doubt patronizing and even paternalistic, but nonetheless understandable. We conclude that the strong overrepresentation of women in the NOHSAP treatment conditions probably resulted from the well-known lifeboat effect: women and children first.

Further examination of more than a hundred additional demographic, background, and behavioral variables reinforced the apparent equivalence of the treatment and control groups (data not shown). Aside from the obvious bias against men, the only other significant selection factor emerging in the analysis was that persons with a long history of homelessness were somewhat less likely to be selected for treatment (and, as would be expected, this difference diminished—but did not disappear—with gender controlled). Otherwise, treatment and control groups were statistically indistinguishable on all other variables we examined.

Discussion

From an implementation standpoint, the randomization of clients into treatment was seriously undermined. In retrospect, the conjuncture of active staff sabotage, administrative incompetence, and high turnover on the part of the program staff, coupled with our own naïveté, failure to establish sufficient accountability, and our explicit decision to not intervene in clinical affairs effectively doomed the randomization effort to failure.

Nevertheless, we would argue that the NOHSAP experiment qua experiment was not appreciably challenged, much less rendered the unmitigated disaster one might expect from the data reported in Table 2.1. After all, the intent and goal of randomization is to forestall bias and ensure equivalence. Fortunately, as the data in Table 2.2 and other reported analyses indicate, although the process of randomization may have broken down, the essential equivalence of the treatment and control groups was not seriously undermined once gender is explicitly controlled.

We thus confront the paradox that despite what we now consider to be a concerted effort on the part of the program staff to defeat randomization, the net result was—excepting gender—essentially random assignment. For the first few months, we were naïvely willing to believe that the pangs of rapid organizational growth, high program staff demands, and frequent staff turnover simply made communication and documentation processes difficult and that things would sort themselves out. Moreover, we were so intent on baselining clients that we did not pay sufficient attention to much else. We thought—mistakenly—that we had a working consensus and that the necessary procedures were in place. We certainly never perceived the need to have the clinical staff account for the outcomes of the randomizations we had undertaken. To have even thought such a thing, much less to have implemented it, struck us as extremely patronizing and distrustful. It violated our sense of partnership.

This is not to say that we were unaware of problems; rather, we mistook profound difficulties for kinks and minor nuisances. Only later did we realize the depths of the problem. By that point, we were even less willing to intervene in the clinical setting; by then, our role as distant evaluators and outside analysts was clearly established and any effort to intervene would have doubtlessly compromised other research objectives. (For a general discussion of roles adopted by evaluators, see Rossi and Freeman, 1989; Shadish and Epstein, 1987.)

At the very beginning of the field stage, it was readily apparent that things were not running smoothly. The clinical staff was constantly shorthanded and often overworked. Staff was often at a loss to define their exact duties and the clinical and administrative demands of their positions. Not surprisingly, there was a noticeable lack of consensus among the program staff as to what specific tasks and responsibilities their jobs entailed. It was clearly an organization in disarray.

The fact that repeated attempts to address these problems, specifically those that affected the research effort (such as randomization), were greeted by direct indications of the program staffs' understanding and willingness to cooperate—though without behavioral effect—would indicate a more active but not necessarily conscious (or, to be exact, passive aggressive) attempt to sabotage the effort to randomize.

What, exactly, went wrong? We thought we had a randomization scheme in place that gave the treatment staff complete control over who would enter the pool for randomization into further treatment and that absolved the treatment staff from any further responsibility for the actual placement once the pool had been determined ("Hey, I tried ... I got you on the list. The computer screwed you, not us"), and finally, a scheme that could be manipulated when the need arose to guarantee a favorable placement for a particular likeable client. Why would the treatment staff sabotage such a congenial and workable system?

The answer, based on our subsequent analysis of the process evaluation data and field notes, is that most of the clinical staff felt that even the determination of suitability required clinical decisions of them that they were not prepared to make. Most of the treatment staff had little experience and less formal training in substance abuse treatment; nearly all were recovering addicts themselves. Many had spent the larger share of their adult lifetimes trying to recover from destructive decisions that affected their own lives and now they were being required to make decisions that would profoundly affect the lives of other people much like them. Given their lack of experience and what can only be described as inadequate clinical supervision, the discomfort of the staff with the determination of eligibility came to be perceived as a personal deficiency whose exposure would at least be an embarrassment and that might lead to formal sanctions or even the loss of their job. Consequently, the staff ended up refusing to make anything but the most obvious and routine judgements about eligibility for further treatment. Clients who did not appear to be "working their program" or who did not exhibit sufficient compliance were deemed ineligible. The remainder went on the randomization lists. In cases where the outcome of randomization produced an unwanted outcome, the randomization was, it appears, simply ignored.

As the program proceeded, lists for randomization were faxed to Tulane regularly. We would do the randomization, pick the "winners," and fax the outcomes back to the program. It never occurred to us that there was yet another step: The program director would look over who had won and who had lost, and then often make decisions about who would be offered a further placement. It was only after the fact, when we were attempting to account for each client's placement in treatment, that it occurred to us to compare the randomization lists against the actual facility census.

In retrospect, much of this seems reducible to the barriers to implementation foreshadowed in our prefield discussions with the clinical staff. In essence, we failed to appreciate staff concerns and to effectively communicate the meaning, the need, and the means for randomization in a wholly non-threatening manner. This was something we thought we appreciated and had sought to address well before the clinical and field phases of NOHSAP commenced. Clearly we had not. But as God is kind to drunks and little children, so too is She kind, apparently, to people like us who study drunks and their little children; in any case, gender aside, some higher power had conspired to create initially equivalent treatment and control groups despite the failure of the randomization process.

References

Devine, J. A., and Wright, J. D. *The Greatest of Evils: Urban Poverty and the American Under-class.* Hawthorne, N.Y.: Aldine de Gruyter, 1993.

Fureman, B., Parikh, G., Bragg, A., and McLellan, A. T. *Addiction Severity Index,* 5th edition. Philadelphia Veteran's Administration, Center for Studies of Addiction, University of Pennsylvania, 1990.

Rodman, H., and Kolodny, R. "Organizational Strains in the Researcher–Practitioner Relationship." In F. G. Caro (ed.), *Readings in Evaluation Research.* New York: Russell Sage, 1977.

Rossi, P. H., and Freeman, H. E. *Evaluation: A Systematic Approach.* Newbury Park, Calif.: Sage Publications, 1989.

Rudegeair, A. *Searching for Shelter: An Analysis of Metropolitan New Orleans' Homeless Programs.* New Orleans, La.: Associated Catholic Charities, 1990.

Shadish, W. R., and Epstein, R. "Patterns of Program Evaluation Practice Among Members of the Evaluation Research Society and Evaluation Network." *Evaluation Review,* 1987, *11,* 555–590.

Sonnichsen, R. C. "Program Managers: Victims or Victors in the Evaluation Process?" In G. Barkdoll and J. Bell (eds.), *Evaluation and the Federal Decision Maker.* New Directions for Program Evaluation, no. 41. San Francisco: Jossey-Bass, 1989.

Weiss, C. H. "Between the Cup and the Lip." In F. G. Caro (ed.), *Readings in Evaluation Research.* New York: Russell Sage, 1977.

Wright, J. D., and Devine, J. A. "Family Backgrounds and the Substance-Abusive Homeless: The New Orleans Experience." *Community Psychologist,* 1993a, *26* (2), 35–37.

Wright, J. D., and Devine, J. A. *The Least of Mine: The New Orleans Homeless Substance Abusers Project Final Report.* New Orleans, La.: Department of Sociology, Tulane University, 1993b.

Wright, J. D., Devine, J. A., and Eddington, N. "The New Orleans Homeless Substance Abusers Project." *Alcoholism Treatment Quarterly,* 1993, *10* (3–4), 51–64.

JOEL A. DEVINE is associate professor of sociology, Tulane University, New Orleans, Louisiana.

JAMES D. WRIGHT is the Favrot professor of human relations, Tulane University.

LAURIE M. JOYNER is a Ph.D. candidate in the department of sociology, Tulane University.

This chapter presents how demoralization arose in a community-based, randomized clinical trial and discusses related threats to validity.

Demoralization and Threats to Validity in Birmingham's Homeless Project

Joseph E. Schumacher, Jesse B. Milby, James M. Raczynski, Molly Engle, Ellen S. Caldwell, James A. Carr

In this chapter, we discuss the threats to validity that arose in a research demonstration project designed to study treatments for homeless persons with substance abuse problems. In particular, we describe what we believe negatively affected the morale and motivation of the clients and staff and posed a threat to the experimental control of the study, hereafter referred to as *demoralization*.

Comparing Substance Abuse Treatments for the Homeless

The Birmingham Homeless Project was a cooperative effort between the Birmingham Health Care Coalition for the Homeless and The University of Alabama at Birmingham School of Medicine. The Health Care Coalition for the Homeless provided project-designed services to the participants and investigators from the university provided scientific oversight.

The intent of the project was to test the efficacy of an enhanced day treatment (enhanced care) by comparing it to currently existing services (usual care) to homeless persons with substance abuse problems. The design used a randomized clinical trial with repeated outcome measures. Enhanced care clients received substantially more frequent, more intense, and therapeutically superior treatment than usual care clients plus drug-free, contingent work rehabilitation and housing. All clients were assessed for changes in substance use, employment, and housing status at three follow-up points.

NEW DIRECTIONS FOR PROGRAM EVALUATION, no. 63, Fall 1994   © Jossey-Bass Publishers

Demoralization

Recruiters exaggerated the already substantial differences between the two interventions by talking up the work and housing components, thereby violating neutral presentation of the different interventions and setting clients up for a win–lose situation.

Clients were randomly assigned to interventions. For the research investigators, the process of randomization was a familiar investigative procedure, but for the clients and service providers, it was an ethically questionable practice. Program staff were uncomfortable with the randomization process.

The failure to maintain neutrality during the recruitment phase by exaggerating the benefits of the enhanced care program over usual care drew undue negative attention to random assignment and set the stage for significant problems with client and staff morale. Complaints of inadequate services and feelings of rejection and resentment were expressed by clients and staff of the usual care program.

Signs of demoralization also emerged in enhanced care clients. Limited funds for salaries and community resistance to drug-free housing for homeless persons significantly delayed the implementation of the work and housing components. The clients became disillusioned with the project.

Program staff responded with efforts to enhance usual care activities and violated the randomization process. Even with close monitoring, a few usual care clients received opportunities reserved for the enhanced care group. Attendance rates significantly declined and an 11 percent increase in cocaine relapse rates for usual care clients was revealed.

Alternative explanations for these effects should be mentioned because this was not a formal study of demoralization. Some of the outcomes mentioned would have been highly likely anyway, given the difference between the two interventions, such as the attendance rates. Enhanced care clients were expected to attend significantly more days per week than usual care clients. An analysis of treatment involvement of usual care clients at the two-month point suggests that they participated minimally and may not have had the opportunity to obtain the benefits of the intervention. Without a significant dose of treatment, there is no reason to expect improvement. Finally, homeless persons generally are struggling with multiple life problems such as poverty, addiction, low self-esteem, and poor health. It is possible that the frustration encountered in the study may have provided a convenient scapegoat for their continued difficulties.

Solutions

It was critical to deliver the work and housing components as promised for the success of the project and the clients' well-being. For work, we identified alternative jobs that could be offered until the housing and renovation problems were solved. Bad Boy Builders, a private contracting company retained by the project to organize and supervise housing refurbishing activities, was called on to generate new job options. For housing, investigators consulted a group of entrepreneurs who were interested in developing drug-free housing for homeless persons of Birmingham. Pioneer Housing was established as a private not-for-profit corporation to take over the locating, purchasing, and managing housing for the project. Housing was acquired by Pioneer Housing for project clients and subsidized by the study.

To cope with the demoralization problem, particularly among the usual care clients and staff, a social networking club called Club Birmingham that joined clients and staff from the usual and enhanced care programs was devised. Monthly social events were scheduled where clients of both programs joined together, socialized, cooked out, and presented testimonials about their progress in treatment. Prizes for attendance in treatment and completed follow-up assessments were awarded in the presence of peers, program staff, and investigators. Usual care clients had equal status with enhanced care clients in Club Birmingham. If the prospect of eliminating demoralization is unrealistic, effective monitoring through process evaluation, staff reports, or instruments that measure the social, motivational, and emotional climate of the therapeutic environment is recommended.

The research project director was assigned to assess the nature of experimental control problems, establish a closer working relationship between research and program staff, and improve compliance with the research protocol. Retraining counseling and research staff in eligibility and randomization procedures and emphasizing the importance of experimental control was conducted. Usual care clients who were receiving enhanced care interventions were removed from these activities or documented as receiving them for future statistical control analyses. Investigators maintained closer contact with the program staff throughout the remainder of the study to provide training and ensure compliance with the research protocol.

Several alternative designs are offered to study the efficacy of treatment interventions that may allay negative effects of random assignment: observational or quasi-experimental designs where process evaluation and within-subject analyses would be the primary determinants of outcome; a delayed-treatment design where the control group eventually enters the enhanced care program; a multiple-baseline design in which outcome effects are measured as various components of enhanced care are added across time; and a randomized two-group design in which the two interventions differ more in concept than in quality.

Conclusions: Threats to Validity

Demoralization represented a potential threat to the validity of this study in a number of ways. First, if the worsening of the usual care clients from baseline to the two-month follow-up point was related to demoralization, there exists a potential for an overestimation of treatment effects of the enhanced care program. Second, if demoralization did significantly contribute to changes in outcome, its effects should be measured and accounted for in the analyses. As recommended earlier in this chapter, monitoring and assessment for threats of this kind would have been useful. Third, a selection bias resulting from differences in characteristics of clients who dropped out (for example, less motivated) versus those who stayed in treatment (more motivated) may well have an effect on outcome not due to the independent variable. Fourth, any changes in the nature or quality of the interventions due to efforts to cope with the demoralization problem, such as Club Birmingham or placement of usual care clients into enhanced care programs, make it difficult to identify specific determinants of outcome.

In conclusion, although the Birmingham Homeless Project was not a study of the effect of demoralization on validity or treatment outcome, we do feel that demoralization had an impact on the clients, staff, and implementation of the study as planned. We consider our observations hypotheses because factors that truly contributed to the final outcome of this study are quite complex and have not been fully explored.

JOSEPH E. SCHUMACHER, JESSE B. MILBY, JAMES M. RACZYNSKI, MOLLY ENGLE, and ELLEN S. CALDWELL are with the University of Alabama at Birmingham School of Medicine.

JAMES A. CARR is clinical director at the Birmingham Health Care for the Homeless Coalition in Birmingham, Alabama.

Issues encountered when using random assignment in social service research are examined. Examples from three social programs are used to illustrate the problems that were encountered and the solutions developed.

Common Implementation Issues in Three Large-Scale Social Experiments

Sally J. Stevens

Random Assignment in Social Service Research

Campbell and Stanley (1966) advocated the use of randomized and quasi-experimental designs in assessing the effects of educational practices. They preferred randomized to quasi-experiments because the latter rule out fewer threats to internal validity. Since then, randomization of subjects to either treatment or a control group has been the most accepted method by which social science researchers attempt to understand the impact of the treatment under study. Although most researchers still agree that the random assingment component in research is important, some have argued that not all research need include random assignment.

In deciding when to use random assignment in a research study, Dennis and Boruch (1989) proposed a set of "threshold" conditions that should be met before considering the randomized design experiment. Researchers should consider whether the random design for their particular study allows for good ethical standards and whether other designs might provide for more accurate answers to the questions under study.

De Leon (1993) states that not all research studies should include randomization. A feasibility study should be conducted first to examine whether a randomized design study could even be carried out and, if so, whether the study would be worthwhile.

This research is supported by three federally funded grants: National Institute on Drug Abuse 1 U01 DA 07470 and 1 R18 DA 06918, and National Institute on Alcohol Abuse and Alcoholism 5 U01 AA08788.

Stevens, Erickson, Chong, and Mullen (1993) argue that although random design allows for causal inferences about program effectiveness, the addition of random assignment may, in fact, significantly alter the program to be studied.

This paper attempts to articulate some of the problems that can occur because of random design. Three large-scale, research-based service programs that use the random design are reviewed. The problems as well as resolutions are discussed.

Amity, Inc. Research Projects

Amity, Inc. is a not-for-profit substance abuse treatment, prevention, and research agency based in Tucson, Arizona. Three of Amity's research projects are the focus of this chapter. A brief description of each project is provided below:

Community Outreach Project on AIDS in Southern Arizona (COPASA). The COPASA project is an HIV research and prevention project funded by the National Institute on Drug Abuse (NIDA). The project uses a street outreach model to recruit eligible injection drug users (IDUs) and crack cocaine users (CCUs) into the study. Eligible adults are given a baseline interview (Risk Behavior Assessment) that assesses their HIV risk. The participants are then randomly assigned to either a standard or a more intensive experimental HIV risk-reduction intervention. A Risk Behavior Follow-up Assessment is given at six months to determint whether HIV risk behavior has decreased and, if so, in what way and for whom.

Addicted Mother and Offspring in Recovery (AMOR). The AMOR project is a drug treatment research project funded by NIDA. The project provides women who have children with long-term residential drug treatment in a therapeutic community (TC) setting. Half of the women are randomly assigned to have their children with them in treatment and half are randomly assigned to have their children placed in another setting, such as state foster care or with a relative, while they are in treatment. The women are assessed on various alcohol/drug and psychological measures at baseline and on a quarterly basis while in the program. Follow-ups are conducted at six, twelve, and twenty-four months after discharge.

Amity Settlement Services for Education and Transition (ASSET). The ASSET project is a substance abuse treatment and research project funded by the National Institute on Alcohol Abuse and Alcoholism (NIAAA). The project provides short-term substance abuse treatment for homeless adults in a TC setting. Participants are randomly assigned to either a four-month highly structured residential TC or a four-month day-treatment nonresidential TC. A baseline interview, in-treatment assessments, and posttreatment follow-up assessments similar to that of the AMOR project are administered.

Acceptance of Random Assignment by Treatment and Intervention Staff. The clinical staff in each of the research projects had difficulty accepting the random assignment protocol. In the COPASA project, participants varied in terms of their HIV risk behaviors and in their willingness to change their behavior. Staff expressed concern about not being able to spend more time with participants who were assigned to the control group and who also exhibited extreme high-risk behavior or expressed a strong desire to be helped.

Staff at the AMOR program felt that the decision about which mothers would be allowed to bring their children into treatment with them should be a clinical decision dependent upon the alternative living situation for the children and the behavior of the mother. In some cases, the children had good alternative placements, such as a caring family member. Others relied upon the state foster care system and still others had difficulty finding placements for their children. In this study, the random assignment left little room for the living situation of the children to be a factor in the assignment of the mother. The random assignment also did not allow for the mother to demonstrate behavior that might be rewarded by having her children come to live with her in treatment. This inability to reward a woman's growth and positive behavior troubled the clinical staff. In a TC environment, motivation is a crucial ingredient; appropriate behavior such as participating in group and taking care of other residents is rewarded. With this random design, women who just "got by" were as likely to have their children assigned into treatment with them as women who worked toward recovery. Consequently, a critical treatment element, motivation, is lost.

The ASSET staff also had a difficult time with the random assignment. Often, the life situation of a given participant made her more appropriate for one component. For example, if shelter beds for women were full and a woman was randomly assigned to the nonresidential component, she would not have a safe place to spend her nights. Even though not being in the program meant the same outcome (no overnight housing), this lack of control haunted the clinical staff. Consequently, women in this predicament who sought out the ASSET project were referred to another Amity program that could provide them with safe housing. This solution seemed the most ethical way for the Amity ASSET project to handle the problem and a critical lesson about designing randomized experiments was learned. Entrance criteria for treatment programs that use the random design may have to be more restrictive in their entrance criteria than programs that use client matching or direct assignment to treatment components. In this case, the entrance criteria had to be restricted to allow for the clients' safety. Although ability to generalize externally was restricted, the program's virtue and integrity of "doing the right thing" was upheld.

If program staff do not embrace the random design, they can sabotage the random assignment by not recruiting participants, badmouthing the idea of random assignment so that it negatively affects the morale of other program staff and program participants, and providing the experimental services anyway, thereby creating intervention slippage. Thus, the first task of the program director is to ensure that the staff members accept random assignment as part of the program and as part of their job. In the three Amity projects, it took varying lengths of time for each program's staff to accept the random design. The COPASA staff were the least resistant, in part because the participants generally did not care whether they were randomized into the standard or experimental intervention. In all three projects, several steps were taken to help program staff embrace the random design.

Team Approach. It is important that lead research and program staff work together and agree on the program guidelines and the research design, particularly the random assignment. The program and research directors should make policy decisions (such as entrance criteria, dropout policy, and relapse policy) together. Critical to a good working relationship between program and research staff is cooperation and a united front by the lead staff. If the relationship between lead staff is viewed as being divisible, all policy, guidelines, and procedures become, at some level, divisible.

Hiring and Training Practices. In all three of the Amity projects, the random design is discussed with applicants when they apply for a position. Explanation of the random procedure is part of the interview and potential staff are made aware that working with this design is not for everyone. Once employed, staff need to be reminded that the random design is not optional. The times when the randomized design was questioned by lead staff were the times when the AMOR and ASSET projects evidenced the most problems with the random design. Random design was never questioned by COPASA lead staff and fewer problems with the acceptance of the design resulted.

Ongoing training on research technology helps program staff appreciate research and understand its usefulness for program evaluation and development. The random design takes away the direct care staff's decision-making authority about which program component the participant should be assigned. This is troublesome to counselors who really want to work in the best interest of their client and who hold an opinion about what is best for their client. Thus, every attempt must be made to increase staff awareness of the benefits of the random design so that they are more comfortable with the procedure.

Whenever possible, research staff should present enlightening information that resulted from the use of random designs in other studies. Furthermore, research staff should provide feedback to the program staff on a regular basis. At Amity, this feedback loop has sparked a number of exciting conversations in which research staff present data and the program staff discuss why they think the data look as they do. Lead program and research staff seem to benefit as much from these discussions as the direct care and research staff, as important theoretical concepts are touched upon, implications for program strategies emerge, and ideas for future research are elucidated.

Services. Direct care staff should be made aware that although participants may not be assigned to a particular component, participants still receive services that may result in equally good treatment outcomes. Reductions in the number of people on waiting lists for treatment and reduction in time that people must wait for treatment are also positive outcomes of the project being implemented. Additionally, in setting up the study one can include "compassionate slots" allowing a certain number of placements to be directly assigned (not randomly assigned) to a particular condition. It must be remembered, however, that these participants are not research subjects, and must be treated separately in the data base. This strategy was used in the AMOR project and proved to take the bite out of the random design. Staff saved the two compassionate slots for women who had extraordinary circumstances such as having no place for their children to live or being HIV-positive.

Presentation of the Random Assignment to Potential Clients. It is difficult to explain the random assignment design to people seeking HIV prevention or drug treatment services. Particularly in the AMOR and ASSET projects, people seeking treatment often express desire to be in one of the two components. Almost all of the mothers in the AMOR program wanted to have their children live with them. The ASSET participants were mixed: Some wanted residential and others wanted the nonresidential component.

Staff grappled with how to explain the random assignment to potential participants, how to actually perform the random assignment, and who should be present when the randomization is facilitated. After years of trial and error, it was concluded that potential participants should be told very simply that the project is a research project and be told what is involved in each of the components to which they may be assigned. This is done twice, first by the program staff and later by the research staff. Program staff explain that no one has control over the assignment; rather, the assignment is like a lottery. Explanation of the random assignment is again reviewed by the research staff just before the signing of the consent form and the baseline interview.

How random assignment is conducted is important. Randomization should be generated by a computer or by a table of random numbers so that the assignment of the participant to a condition is depersonalized. The assignments are done in advance and placed in sealed envelopes. In the projects in which the participants express strong desire for one component over another, this method takes away any personal responsibility. For example, for the mothers at the AMOR project who wanted their children to live with them in treatment, hand-picking the "wrong" slip of paper might make them feel (unfairly so) responsible for the living situation of their children.

In projects where the assignment is important to the participant, both a research staff member and a program person (either staff or senior participant) should be with the participant at the opening of the envelope that contains the random assignment. The research staff should give the participant the envelope so that the program staff are removed from any connection with the assignment. Thus, program staff bias for or against a participant is alleviated. A program person should be present for the emotional support of the participant who is being randomized.

Problems Encountered with Referring Agencies Because of Random Assignment.   In both the AMOR and ASSET programs, staff from referring agencies had difficulty with the random design even though finding residential placements for mothers and children or homeless adults was difficult when the Amity projects began. Referring staff wanted to choose the component to which their client would be placed. The random assignment took away their ability to do what they thought was clinically right for their client. For the ASSET project, discussions with executive and program directors who supported Amity's research projects did not help to increase referrals. Only when the direct care staff of each agency were contacted and educated about the project did referrals begin to occur. This took an enormous amount of work, but increases in the number of referrals did result. Because enrollment was still lower than expected, the ASSET staff also began to conduct street outreach to soup kitchens, parks, and other areas where homeless adults hang out. Sixty-three percent of those enrolled in the ASSET project came from this street outreach effort.

Staff at the AMOR project also conducted street outreach to improve enrollment. However, this method did not prove to be effective, perhaps because drug-using mothers with children are a more hidden population compared with homeless men and women. AMOR staff then extended their referral network to include agencies that served women who had already lost custody of their children or who were on the verge of losing their children. Thus, more emphasis was placed on working with the legal system (probation officers, parole officers, judges, and jail personnel). Offering the random assignment (a 50 percent chance to have their children) to women who had lost or were going to lose custody of their children was attractive and referrals began to occur.

Intervention Slippage.   In all three of these research projects, concern about intervention slippage existed. In the COPASA and AMOR projects, the same staff facilitated both the standard and experimental interventions. At COPASA, it was thought that the intervention staff may at times provide more than the standard care to those randomly assigned to the standard. Separate staff were not assigned for each intervention because of funding constraints and because the lead staff were not convinced that this division of labor was needed to ensure rigidity of the two interventions. Instead, a detailed manual outlining the contents of the two interventions was developed. Staff were asked to use specific cue cards and handouts, thereby forcing more compliance in the intervention delivery. Documentation of the exact time a participant is involved in the intervention, the referrals given, and any problems (client was high on drugs; client did not pay attention) are recorded by the intervention staff and added to the data base by the research staff.

Occasionally at the COPASA project, a couple will enroll in the program. In this case, the couple is randomly assigned to one of the two conditions as data from previous Amity projects indicated that couples, housemates, and bunkmates in jail share information obtained during the intervention.

Although the sample size is reduced, the integrity of the intervention is retained.

The ASSET project showed evidence of intervention slippage, but from a source different than expected. Intervention slippage in this program occurred when the nonresidential male participants self-organized and developed a quasi-residential living arrangement. Several attempts at organization were made. First, the nonresidential male participants obtained permission from a shelter director to stay together in one area (corner) of the shelter. Later, another group of nonresidential men were given permission by a church leader to sleep on the back porch of the church. A third group of nonresidential men organized and set up a sleeping arrangement in the alley next to the nonresidential site, which later became known as the Oasis. This type of organization is a critical element that is taught in a TC model; client A helps client B and together they build community, pulling together in their recovery. To forbid this organization would be equivalent to telling the participants they could not do what they were taught to do in their educational and group intervention sessions. Thus, a decision was made to allow the participants to self-organize and to make necessary adjustments in the data analysis allowing for the comparison of three groups (residential, nonresidential, and a quasiresidential group).

Some intervention slippage occurred in the AMOR project. Women who were not randomly assigned to have their children in treatment were allowed visits with their children. There was a tendency to arrange for frequent visitation for women who did not get to have their children in treatment with them. Consequently, the two groups (women with their children and women without their children) began to look more alike. In response, specific guidelines regarding visitation were developed and, consequently, more control over the visitation variable was evidenced. Additionally, all visitations were documented, so the amount of time women spent with their children is a variable that can be examined.

Impact of Changes in Participant Status. All programs experience changes in the status of their participants. Some participants do not show up for treatment, others drop out of treatment, and still others may be terminated for breaking program rules or for other reasons. In nonresearch-based programs, staff simply open up the treatment slot for another individual. In research-based programs that randomly assign participants to various conditions, one cannot just place another individual into the opening.

In the ASSET program, the differential attrition rate from the residential program along with the fact that the residential program could not handle as many participants caused problems for the random assignment design. Residential treatment slots were often full while attendance in the nonresidential component was not always at full capacity. Fortunately, in planning the project, lead staff reviewed dropout rates for similar programs and, based upon these rates, designed the ASSET project so that two-thirds of the participants would be assigned to the nonresidential component and one-third would be assigned to the residential component. Despite this prior planning, the winter mont hs evidenced openings at the nonresidential site while the residential site remained full. Project staff had two choices: Stop enrollment until random assignment could be facilitated or suspend random assignment and offer potential participants the nonresidential component. Because the TC model uses the group process, it is imperative that a sufficient number of participants be enrolled. To maintain the integrity of the treatment model, direct assignment into the nonresidential component was the lesser of two evils. Additionally, an upper limit of forty was established for the nonresidential component; all enrollment would stop if the residential component was full and the nonresidential component had forty participants. Research staff kept track of the individuals who were not randomly assigned so that later analysis of the data could take this into account.

Implications of Practice, Research, and Policy

In reviewing the issue of random design in these three Amity research projects, some conclusions can be made. First, it is imperative that program and research personnel form a team, particularly those that direct the project. Secondly, staff training should be ongoing and a feedback loop between program and research staff must be developed and ongoing. Third, not only should executive and program directors from referring agencies be informed about the project, but a significant amount of time should be spent educating the direct care staff of other agencies about the project, particularly the random assignment design. Fourth, alternative recruitment strategies must be considered if enrollment is lower than originally anticipated.

The research design must allow for concessions, whether that means restricting the entrance criteria, including direct assignment to compassionate slots before randomization, allowing participants to slip the intervention when it fits with the treatment model, or suspending the random assignment when one component is full or when couples enroll in the program together. Furthermore, random assignment should not be glossed over; rather, the random design and what that means for the participant should be explained to the participant at least twice before their assignment. When the assignment takes place, both a research staff member and a program person should be present.

The positive aspects that the randomized design brings to research must be weighed against the problems it may create. In developing a random design study, one must think through the problems and possible alternatives or solutions. Some questions that should be raised before developing a study include whether both of the assigned conditions provide good alternative treatment choices, whether both conditions provide for more than the usual services provided in the wider community, and what treatment alternatives are possible if eligible prospective participants cannot participate for safety reasons or other legitimate reasons.

In designing the research, one should consider blocking, that is, randomly assigning people within subgroups, on variables of particular importance. One might also consider using different rates of assignment or using multiple stages of randomization. Furthermore, in examining what went on during the treatment period, it is important to measure both intended and unintended treatment for both the standard and experimental groups. Finally, researchers must also realize that what seems like a simple addition of the random assignment procedure might significantly alter the very program or treatment model they intended to study. Results from studies that include the random design must be interpreted very carefully, as the program that was studied may have been changed not only by the addition of the random design but by the characteristics of the people willing to participate.

References

Campbell, D. T., and Stanley, J. C. *Experimental and Quasi-Experimental Designs for Research.* Skokie, Ill.: Rand McNally, 1966.

De Leon, G. Discussant at the Therapeutic Community Association/Center for Therapeutic Community Research; Symposium on Therapeutic Community Research Designs/Random Assignment: Issues and Solutions, May 24, 1993.

Dennis, M. L., and Boruch, R. F. "Randomized Experiments for Planning and Testing Projects in Developing Countries: Threshold Conditions." *Evaluation Review,* 1989, *13,* 292–309.

Stevens, S. J., Erickson, J. R., Chong, J., and Mullen, R. "ASSET: Research Design, Implications and Modifications." Presented at the Therapeutic Community Association/Center for Therapeutic Community Research; Symposium on Therapeutic Community Research Designs/Random Assignment: Issues and Solutions, May 24, 1993.

SALLY J. STEVENS is director of research for Amity, Inc., a nonprofit substance abuse treatment, prevention, and research therapeutic community in Tucson, Arizona. She is also principal Investigator for Amity's COPASA (NIDA), AMOR (NIDA), and ASSET (NIAAA) research projects.

Some of the practical difficulties encountered when using an experimental design involving human subjects with multiple serious needs are outlined. Suggestions are given for dealing effectively with these difficulties, and the chapter provides further critical commentary.

"I Prayed Real Hard, So I Know I'll Get In": Living with Randomization

Julie A. Lam, Stephanie Wilson Hartwell, James F. Jekel

The New Haven Project was one of fourteen research demonstration projects funded by the National Institute for Alcohol Abuse and Alcoholism (NIAAA) in cooperation with the National Institute for Drug Abuse (NIDA) in their second round of projects funded through the Stewart B. McKinney Act. The projects were designed to evaluate the effectiveness of various treatment models for homeless substance abusers. The New Haven Project focused on homeless men who primarily used cocaine. As with most of the other demonstration projects, this project employed an experimental design, randomly assigning homeless men with cocaine and other substance abuse problems to one of two groups: *the experimental condition,* known as the Grant Street Partnership (GSP), consisting of an intensive ninety-day residential program integrated with nine months of case-management and other ambulatory services, or *the control condition,* receiving the usual community services. The project is described in detail elsewhere (Leaf and others, 1993).

Implementing a randomized clinical trial for homeless substance abusers in New Haven, given the history of tension between the community and the academy (Yale University), was challenged by local service providers and city officials from the beginning. According to one of the original grant writers:

The authors acknowledge the helpful comments of the editor, anonymous reviewers, and of Paul Johnston, Kenneth Thompson, Ariel Martinez, the New Haven Project Research Team, and community service providers in New Haven.

The discussion around randomization and the concerns around this issue for the potential clients, community, and concern about Yale is one of the things among others that fueled the idea of "partnership" . . . the emphasis on the community coming together. Although we are adding something to the community there was a real self-consciousness about the randomization from the beginning.

Furthermore, comments by the clinical director of the local detoxification center sum up many of these concerns:

I question the validity of a control group in the community-based setting, it's not a laboratory. . . . [W]hat we do when we intervene with the community must be in the best interest of the community. . . . [I]t leaves a bitter taste that research drives the process so they can be successful at getting the data they need. The community should drive the process. Once the researchers leave, after they finish publishing their papers, the community is still there.

The relationship between the city of New Haven and Yale University has been one of contentious codependence over the years. The University is involved in many social service endeavors in the city, but there is usually a research string attached, particularly in the provision of health services. The money is provided if the participants are willing to provide data. The fact that this research demonstration project employed an experimental design was a source of tension from the beginning. Attempts were made to find other designs, including one that would compare two treatments—a residential program and a nonresidential program with services. These were rejected because the research designs lacked clarity and conciseness, there was not enough money to fund them, and because of the small size of the city and the limited number of potential research subjects.

The decision to use an experimental design in the face of concerns about possible exploitation of this mostly African-American and Latino population was rationalized in three ways: The control group would be receiving customary or usual services in a community with a highly developed substance abuse treatment system and homeless services, although there are waiting lists of up to six months for the former; there was no evidence that the GSP program would be especially beneficial for all cocaine-abusing homeless men, and the argument might even be made that other types of services would be more beneficial for some men; and it was expected that the project would have a beneficial effect on the system of services in the community, improving services and access to services for this population (the NIAAA was concerned that this might contaminate the research outcomes). In addition, the random assignment of subjects to treatment and control groups has a long tradition of being the most desirable social science research design to test hypotheses about intervention programs (Campbell and Stanley, 1966). Although not required by the funding agency, the grant writers felt that the experimental design was the design most likely to be funded.

From the start, the randomization of subjects to experimental and control groups posed challenges for everyone involved. In fact, one of the first decisions made by the project's executive committee was to come up with another name for the control group, because *control* was thought to have negative connotations reminiscent of the Tuskegee experiments. It was decided to call this condition either *usual care* or *usual services*.

Early discussions among project staff regarding randomization mostly concerned the possible impact randomization might have on the men assigned to the usual care group. It subsequently became clear, however, that randomization was affecting *all* staff involved in the project, from community service providers who served as referral sources to the GSP staff and the research staff. In addition to concerns about the negative emotional impact of randomization on participants and staff, concerns about the integrity of the random assignment arose. Below we discuss each of these concerns, how they manifested themselves, and how the project struggled to overcome them.

Impact of Randomization on the Subjects

Originally, the primary concern of the research staff as well as the community service providers was that randomization might have a negative effect on the usual care group subjects. Fetterman (1982) refers to the group receiving no services in such a design as a "negative treatment group or a reactive control group." Cook and Campbell (1979) call this "resentful demoralization of respondents receiving less desirable treatments."

The research staff was also concerned that randomization might have an extra halo-like effect on the GSP subjects, thus exaggerating any true benefit that might result from the program. In other words, randomization might amplify the apparent effects of the treatment program. Fetterman (1982) reported that students entering an educational program through random assignment felt that they had won a competition, thus producing another treatment effect separate from the so-called program treatment.

These issues were explored through the ethnographic component of the research project. Semistructured interviews with both experimental and usual care group men were done over lunch or in other informal settings. Conversations with men in both groups also took place during the course of field work in the city shelters. Semistructured interviews with community service providers and with research staff were also conducted.

The interviews with the usual care group subjects suggested that there was considerable variation in the extent to which the men were affected by their random assignment. Responses to probes in this area can be classified under several themes.

Some men believed that if they had not gotten into GSP, that they somehow must not have been eligible after all. This was despite careful explanation of the randomization process to them at the time of their baseline interview. One subject who was at risk of homelessness and, therefore, eligible for the project, gave the following explanation for not being selected:

> Well, they told me I had to qualify, but I didn't qualify because I was liv- ing at home and you had to be a homeless person or a street person. . . . yeah, they turned me down.

Other men were philosophical, deciding that it was really for the best because they thought the program sounded too confining. A number of men signed up for the project because it was a sure way to get into a detoxifica- tion unit. They had no intention of going to a ninety-day residential treat- ment program. When asked how he felt about not getting into Grant Street, one man said:

> I wouldn't want a ninety-day program anyway . . . I don't like being locked down. . . . when I was in Dutcher Hall (a detox program) I liked it, but five days was enough.

Another man in the usual care group indicated that he did not know much about the project before going to detox:

> They sent me (to detox). They said it would be good for me to go. I was too f———d up to know the difference.

Some men decided it must have been "the Lord's will" and, therefore, the right thing for them. These men tended to seek one of the alternative com- munity programs. One such man was interviewed about his feelings regarding being in the usual care group while he was concurrently in a VA treatment pro- gram. When asked what he had heard about the Grant Street program while in detox, he replied:

> Yeah, they told me about GSP but they turned me down for whatever rea- sons . . . they said that I was already turned down before they even came out to interview me. They said that the number that was assigned to the person to interview me had that preselection already attached to it. So they knew that this number wasn't going to be honored in the program and . . . that they would interview me anyway and later they would call back and say "no." I just figured that it wasn't for me because I'm relying on the guy (Jesus Christ). . . . at any rate I knew that the Lord was guiding my steps. I knew that I wasn't going to be anywhere that he wouldn't have me to be. . . so if I couldn't understand something or things weren't working out, I'd say thank you, Lord. Because I know he has it all under control.

Another man in the usual care group went to the Salvation Army program when he did not get into Grant Street. He said:

> My name was put in a hat . . . when he (the outreach worker) came to pick me up he said it's not happening, you're not going there . . . I was trying to gain some spirituality on my own, and I was saying I'm going to put it in God's hands. Whatever happens I'm going to go through with it . . . give the Salvation Army a chance.

Other men appeared to understand the lottery-type process, but did not necessarily like it. Instead they were angered:

> [S]he was telling me about the program and there was this thing about they put five pieces of paper in a hat . . . which I don't know who came up with that idea. . . . because here I am going to detox thinking that I'm getting ready to get into a program to better myself . . . I think I could have really made it there, you know. And then after the game was played like I was a guinea pig or something. That pisses me off. Then I really became stuck on that f——ing attitude.

Another man, referring to what he thought was a computer-generated random assignment, asked,

> How can a computer tell me whether or not I need treatment?

When asked how being randomized to the usual care group actually affected their lives, the men were realistic. One man said:

> You can't miss what I didn't have. . . . I mean I just never had it to miss it. It just wasn't there for me period. It was like another closed door.

Another man replied:

> I don't know. I have no way of knowing that. That's something I'll never know. But I know what affects my life is the decisions I make, irregardless of where I am.

Furthermore, several men had had this type of experience before, perhaps a function of research saturation in New Haven or in this particular population. A man in the usual care group, also a participant in a VA research project, had this to say:

> I mean it seems like every time I want a program the research part gets all confused with all these numbers and I don't get in to the good side . . . it (the research) just gets in my way.

The service providers were also concerned about possible demoralization in the usual care group caused by the randomization process. According to the recruitment coordinator:

> They are second-class citizens, but part of the research. . . . It leaves a sour taste. . . . Grant Street is the palace on the hill and the men take this chance to get in, but in reality one group gets serviced, the others are second-class citizens. There are two populations—one that doesn't really care (if they get in) and one that does and would give me their first born if they got in.

A case manager in one of the city shelters had this to say about the effect of randomization on the men in the usual care group:

> I don't like it when someone comes to you and admits that they have a problem finally, that they need help, and they are randomized out. Even if you have something set up for them it does something to them, sometimes they leave. . . . They take the randomization personally. . . . They think that at the interview they answered the questions wrong. They even dress themselves up for the interview.

It should be noted that the usual care group men were offered the opportunity to participate in the research project (initial and follow-up interviews) with the potential to earn up to $140 in total, so that most of them still felt they were gaining something tangible by being part of the research effort. This may have minimized any resentment that otherwise might have appeared.

> Yeah, that definitely helps (the money) . . . that's a plus. . . . I guess I don't know for anybody else, but I probably would have been less receptive if it hadn't been for the monetary reward. . . . Well, I'm just being honest about it.

According to the project's tracker, who was also a volunteer outreach worker on the streets:

> To them it's easy money, easier than stealing . . . another kind of subsidy. . . . The subjects see it like a job, they are selling something. . . . His information is a commodity. . . . If they don't get in it's not a tragedy, it's just more of the same, they don't personalize it.

In addition, the randomization process per se did not appear to have been a major positive factor in the lives of the men who were assigned to the GSP, except that they were able to get into the program. It might be expected that, given a halo-like effect, even the subjects assigned to GSP who dropped out would do better than the usual care group. Early analysis revealed that the men who dropped out of the GSP were very similar to the men in the usual care group on the major outcome variables at the time of the three- and six-month follow-ups. This provides some evidence that merely being assigned to the treatment group did not produce a halo effect, at least not one that lasted for three months.

Our analysis suggests that the randomization process had a less uniformly negative impact on the homeless men assigned to the usual care group than the research staff and community service providers had feared. However, it appears that the randomization process had a stronger negative emotional effect on the staff and service providers than expected.

Impact on the Community Service Providers

Although some of the initial concerns about the effects of the randomization process on the study subjects were allayed, randomization proved to have a major impact on the referral process from the community and on the project's relationships with service providers, especially those from the other homeless shelters.

Most referrals came from homeless shelters in New Haven. Initially, all referrals were to go to the South Central Rehabilitation Center (SCRC), a community-based detoxification and treatment agency in New Haven. However, SCRC was in the process of building its facility and the opening was delayed (SCRC opened in March of 1993). Fortunately, SCRC had linkages with drug and alcohol detoxification programs in several hospitals in Connecticut. Through these linkages, they developed the Bridge Program, which was to operate until their facility opened. The Bridge Program consisted of SCRC finding a detoxification bed for men referred to the project and transporting them to and from the facility. The baseline interview and randomization took place on about the third day of detoxification.

Referrals were slower than expected during the first six months of the program and were not increasing as the program became more established. There were only nineteen referrals from December 1, 1991, through January 31, 1992. The project asked one of the ethnographers to see whether she could determine what was discouraging referrals from the shelters. She discovered that the staff in community shelters were very unhappy with the randomization process; one even claimed that eight referrals she had made were randomized out of GSP. Because the research staff knew this was not true, they obtained the list of eight names from the shelter service provider and found that of the eight, only two were known to the research project (and they *had* both been assigned to the usual care group); the other six referrals had inexplicably been lost somewhere in the process of getting assessed for detoxification and taken to detoxification. Randomization was automatically blamed for a flaw in the referral process.

It became clear that the fact that the research project employed an experimental design did not sit well with these service providers. One case manager in a city shelter remarked:

> I just understood it was research until I actually had to do it with the guys. . . . It bothers me more to know the environment of the program and realize that certain guys' needs fit that program (GSP) rather than work-fare at the Salvation Army. . . . I hate it when I know two people going in at the same time, one person that is not ready, and one that is cooperative and ready, the one that is ready won't get in. . . . It's that Grant Street is so different that guys want to go. I don't know if the word is out that Grant Street has the best wide-screen TV or what, who knows, all I know is Grant Street has this image of a savior place that if they don't get in they don't want anything.

Staff members from the referring agencies were also upset with the many changes in the referral process that were needed to try to meet everyone's needs and make the Bridge Program work. They felt that the process was changing almost daily and they could not keep up with what was required of them to make a referral. One case manager put it like this:

> I don't remember the last formal letter, but there is a change every week, something new to be added. This project is more footwork and gas work than any other project I've ever worked on. . . . TB test, medical clearance, a urine, city welfare. . . . They (GSP) have three vans, but I'm the one who is running around and I'm tired, I like the way it is on paper, but the actual process is not working.

Following extensive discussions with shelter staff, the referral process was changed so that the research office, rather than SCRC, was the first point of contact for referrals. A recruitment coordinator was hired by the research staff (SCRC had been in charge of recruitment). Not only was the recruitment coordinator easier to contact, but also an answering machine provided a place to leave a referral message on evenings, weekends, and the rare time when no research staff member was in the office. By knowing of all referrals, the research staff could ensure that the referred men got into the system if appropriate.

The improvement in referrals was seen in an increase in the average number of referrals per month: Up through March 1992, the average was fourteen referrals per month, and after April 1992 it increased to twenty-six per month. The relationships with shelter providers became less strained and, although they still were not happy with the idea of randomization, they knew that men they referred would not be lost in the system.

Impact on Research Staff

The use of an experimental design in social research, especially dealing with a population of homeless substance abusers, posed problems for the research staff as well. To persons trained in social science research, especially evaluation research, the experimental design is desirable. However, it soon became clear that the design would be difficult to implement.

In a small project such as the one in New Haven, research staff became closely linked with the program and were often seen as service providers by the subjects and their families. There were a number of instances when the project director was begged by research subjects, their family members, and even employees of the program to bend the rules of randomization "just this once." The project director described it this way:

> Several times I have sat in my office with a family member of the client while he is being interviewed across the hall. They tell me all their troubles and how desperate they are for help. Then he comes out, they leave, and I have to do the randomization. I am the one who draws the number to see if they get in or not.

The interviewers were also affected by the randomization process, because they had the job of explaining the randomization process to the men as they obtained informed consent to participate in the research project. They were very careful to explain that the men were still part of the research project even if they did not get into the program. The interviewers were adamantly opposed to being told the outcome of the randomization before the interview was complete and the subject had been informed of the outcome by someone else. They were very uncomfortable with having the responsibility of breaking the news to a man assigned to the usual care group on those few occasions when it was necessary for them to do so.

Changing the Randomization Process to Accommodate the Program

A final concern surrounding the issue of randomization was the necessity of changing the process a number of times throughout the first year of the project. The research staff was concerned that these changes would jeopardize the integrity of the experimental design. Following is a description of the changes that were made and the explanations for those changes.

The GSP program was brand new, opening on July 1, 1991, about nine months after receiving the NIAAA funding. The first twelve eligible men referred to the project were accepted into GSP without being randomized, in order to get the program going. On July 9, 1991, randomization began and was carried out on a 1:1 ratio. On August 12, the ratio was changed to two out of three assigned to the experimental group because of the small number of men in the program. By September, the warm summer weather, the newness of the program, and the uncertainty of referral sources led to a total of only thirty-eight referrals to the GSP, many of whom left almost immediately, partly because of the small number of clients in the program. In order to enable the GSP to build up an ongoing program, the research project requested permission from NIAAA to suspend randomization for three months until the program had developed a critical mass, had achieved stability, and had begun to establish a credible track record in the community. Permission was granted, and randomization was suspended on September 9, 1991.

By late fall 1991, these objectives had been achieved, and the research project again initiated randomization on December 6, 1991. Thereafter, the randomization was kept at a 1:1 experimental:control ratio, although for two months in the spring of 1992 (March 2–May 6) the program numbers dropped seriously and the ratio was changed to 3 GSP:1 control. After that time, the randomization ratio remained at 1:1. After intake for the evaluation component was completed on February 28, 1993, randomization was discontinued and all eligible men were admitted to the GSP if there was space.

Because of these changes in the randomization ratio, it was with some concern that the research staff looked at a comparison of the baseline characteristics of the GSP clients and the usual care group clients. One reason for concern was that if there were seasonal trends in the characteristics of men referred and randomized, changing the ratio might change the baseline characteristics of the two groups. Nevertheless, a comparison of the final sample of 182 subjects in the GSP group and 112 subjects in the usual care group on 58 demographic, substance abuse, housing, incarceration, and psychiatric history items suggested that all was well because there were no more statistically significant differences between the groups than would be expected by chance alone. A closer comparison of the men who were randomized with those who were not on the same 58 baseline variables also revealed only a small number of statistically significant differences. Thus the research team was encouraged that, despite temporary suspension of randomization and changing the randomization ratio to help the program, the two groups to be compared were similar at baseline, though of different size.

Conclusions

We learned a number of lessons from implementing a randomized experiment in a social services setting. First, the randomization process affected different research subjects in different ways. For some, it was not an emotional trauma, as feared. They accepted the results philosophically. Others were not concerned, and were probably actually relieved with the result because they were not interested in a long-term treatment program. Finally, some men were angered by the randomization process and outcome Service providers were much more likely to think that the men in the usual care group were demoralized than the men indicated.

The randomization process did confuse and anger the referral agencies, however. Very serious attention needs to be paid to explaining and re-explaining the randomization process and the importance of using an experimental design to all relevant parties both before the start of the project and throughout the project's existence. This barrier can be overcome only if close attention is paid to the feelings and reactions of all community service providers involved in the project. Even after a great deal of discussion and compromise, negative feelings still exist toward the use of a random clinical trial design with this population.

Randomization did place strains on the research staff and between research and program staff. It is important to maintain one trustworthy person in charge of the actual random assignment. There are many temptations, usually for very compelling reasons, to make exceptions and bend the process for individual subjects. It would probably have been preferable to computerize the process of random assignment and thus take some stress off the project director.

Because the interviewers and recruitment coordinator are on the front lines and are most directly responsible for explaining the randomization process to the subjects and to referral sources, they need to be well-informed about the benefits of experimental design and how the randomization process works. Relieving the interviewers of the responsibility of the actual random assignment and informing the subject of the outcome made good sense, in retrospect. The interviewers were able to maintain more objectivity and felt less emotional stress.

We also learned that changes in the ratio of randomization to GSP and usual care groups, which were made to assist in program development, did not undermine the equivalence of the two groups at baseline. This is important knowledge for other researchers working with experimental designs in the community. It may be necessary to make compromises for the good of the program, and it is comforting to know that these changes do not always jeopardize the baseline comparability of the groups.

Randomization presented a myriad of problems for a new community social intervention. It caused stress and often distress in nearly every phase of the project. Most of these problems could be addressed, however, through careful attention to the concerns of all players: the subjects themselves, the community service providers, and the research staff.

References

Campbell, D. T., and Stanley, J. C. *Experimental and Quasi-Experimental Designs for Research.* Skokie, Ill.: Rand McNally, 1966.

Cook, T. D., and Campbell, D. T. *Quasi-Experimentation: Design and Analysis Issues for Field Settings.* Chicago: Rand McNally, 1979.

Fetterman, D. M. "Ibsen's Baths: Reactivity and Insensitivity (A Misapplication of the Treatment–Control Design in a National Evaluation)." *Educational Evaluation and Policy Analysis,* 1982, *4* (3), 261–79.

Leaf, P. J., and others. "Partnerships in Recovery: Shelter-Based Services for Homeless Cocaine Abusers: New Haven." *Alcoholism Treatment Quarterly,* 1993, *10* (3–4), 77–90.

JULIE A. LAM was the project director of the New Haven Project and is currently the project director for the national client-level evaluation of the ACCESS Program for severely mentally ill homeless clients at the Northeast Program Evaluation Center of the VA Medical Center, West Haven, Connecticut.

STEPHANIE WILSON HARTWELL was an ethnographer/research assistant with the New Haven Project and is a Ph.D. candidate in the Department of Sociology, Yale University, New Haven, Connecticut.

JAMES F. JEKEL was the principal investigator for the New Haven Project and is the C.E.A. Winslow Professor of Public Health and the director of the Preventive Medicine Residency Program, Yale University School of Medicine, New Haven, Connecticut.

The use of experimental methods in a homeless service initiative confronted a variety of problems not reported by Lam, Jekel, and Hartwell. These include ethical and internal validity issues, organizational problems, effects on the research team itself, and the impact of research as a requirement for services on New Haven's public institutions.

Effects of Randomization on a Homeless Services Initiative: A Comment

Paul Johnston, Patrick Swift

Lam, Hartwell, and Jekel (LHJ) underestimate the impact of experimental methods on a service project for homeless men in New Haven, Connecticut. They obscure important effects of the research apparatus on clients, on relations with other service providers, on the city's network of homeless services and its efforts to strengthen them, and on the research team itself. This episode displays, we argue, a pervasive field of expert power centered in New Haven at Yale University, curiously invisible to itself.

Impact on Clients

LHJ reduce this issue to the threat of "resentful demoralization" among those randomized into the control group and a "halo effect" among those randomized into the treatment group. Using quotes from participants, they argue that resentful demoralization was minimal, mainly because many men didn't understand the randomization process anyway (thus the title, "I Prayed Real Hard, So I Know I'll Get In.")

This problem does not disappear, however, merely because those denied services do not display uniformly resentful demoralization. In fact, these interviews did reveal resentment among some unknown proportion of those applicants.

The authors acknowledge the helpful comments of Michael Rowe and Kendon Conrad.

More important, however, are problems ignored in this account. The first problem is ethical: denial of treatment to applicants for care, regardless of whether the applicant understands the denial as the luck of the draw or "God's will." The original research team and collaborating service providers understood that the network of usual services to which control group members would be assigned was gravely inadequate. The shelter system was viewed as pathogenic, and the substance abuse treatment system as inaccessible to the homeless. We resolved concerns about denial of services to the control group with the judgment that "given the fact that this new program cannot meet the total demand for services of this population . . . the random selection process has been accepted . . . as a fair method of allocating limited resources." (Leaf and Thompson, 1990, p. 50. See also p. 46.) This left us, however, with a clear understanding that if Grant Street were significantly underused, then this ethical issue would rear its head again. For most of the term of the project, GSP *was* significantly underused. Random assignment lasted for twenty months; for the first fifteen of those months, capacity use fluctuated between 35 percent and 75 percent. Only in the final months of the intervention did use remain above 75 percent. (Ironically, as we shall see below, this underuse was apparently caused by procedures intended to facilitate random assignment.)

Also neglected is another effect on clients: false positive self-reports by participants stemming from the absence of a true double-blind experiment. Members of the treatment group knew very well what was expected of them by researchers. As it evolved, the program stressed individuals' moral obligation to stay off drugs, culminating in a ritual in which participants stood before community members—and research team members—to testify about their commitment to stay clean. Not surprisingly, ethnographic evidence later suggested that a significant number of those reporting to the research team that they had remained drug-free were actually using drugs. Despite an extensive literature documenting such false positive self-reports (Hser, Anglin, and Chou, 1988; Mesch and Kandel, 1988), LHJ assume that self-report in formal interviews is more reliable than ethnographic observation, and so disregard this threat to internal validity.

Impact on Service Providers

Describing recruitment difficulties and contentious relations with other service providers, LHJ argue that those service providers inaccurately attributed "flaws in the referral process" to randomization. The program's cumbersome recruitment arrangements—contracted out to another new agency—were indeed a recipe for misunderstanding and conflict. LHJ neglect to note, however, that this mechanism was set up at least in part to allow randomization of applicants before contact with the program. (When recruitment was finally brought in-house, program occupancy picked up considerably.)

Moreover, opposition by community members to the experimental design was based not only on flaws in the referral process but also on several widely shared perceptions: that the New Haven community had served for decades as a laboratory for experimental efforts; that on balance those efforts appeared to have more positive effects on the careers of Yale-based researchers than on the quality of life for community members; and that researchers and their agendas exercised undue power through the community's dependence on research for services. Some service providers argued that randomization provided only an illusion of scientific rigor and that although these methods were unlikely to produce valid results, they invested the project with a mantle of legitimacy that limited its local accountability.

Impact on the Project

LHJ are concerned about whether changes in the randomization process to accommodate the program undermined the experiment. In fact, the changes at issue were required not to accommodate the program but rather to compensate for underuse caused by the randomization process. More important, though, were extensive changes in the program to accommo date the experiment—in response to researcher interests, considerations of experimental design, and the interests of the NIAAA research-and-demonstration effort. For example, what local officials had planned as a resource center for New Haven's homeless—a drug-free environment, not a treatment program, aiming mainly to move homeless men into transitional housing and vocational opportunities—was redefined as a drug treatment program. Then the "resource center" agenda was redefined as "aftercare"; as the aftercare program was never implemented and the project became, in effect, only a drug treatment program, focused on individual pathologies rather than institutional change. Ironically, along with other factors, this also undermined the strength of the clinical program.

Furthermore, NIAAA strictures against interventions that would strengthen the whole system of services (for fear of positive effects on the control group) retarded local plans for broader system integration efforts.

Researchers' interests in homeless mental health systems focused the planning efforts on the intake side of the project—its relationship with homeless shelters and detox facilities—while neglecting resources on the output side such as housing and job training.

Finally, the mantle of scientific legitimacy and the cushion of fiscal support stemming from the project's status as an experimental demonstration project buffered it from local accountability and limited its need for coalition-building and linkage with other agencies. The planning group assembled by researchers exercised effective power over the program during the defining early period of the intervention and then—despite plans for other oversight groups—became the project's sole oversight body. Hesitant to provoke criticism for "Yale interference" and influenced by norms of noninterventionist observation, the research team neglected to hold project managers accountable for radical departures from the program design (most importantly, for failure to develop the external program for former residents). On the conclusion of the NIAAA funding, no structure of accountability or oversight was left in existence. Rather, decisions regarding the future use of the facility moved by default into the hands of the administrators of the agency with whom the city and Yale had originally contracted to operate the program.

In the absence of researchers' intervention and NIAAA funding, would the city have been able to implement its homeless initiative? Possibly not, given the city's fiscal crisis. Although funds were available for purchase and rehabilitation of the site and for shelter staffing, additional support for clinical and case management staff was unlikely without much closer collaboration with other agencies with control over housing, job training and placement, drug treatment, and other resources. In either case, the effort would have faced major barriers to access to external resources for participants after completion of the residential program. On the other hand, had planners and administrators—lacking the luxury of autonomous funding and the mantle of experimental design—been forced to build these relationships, access to those resources and so program outcomes may have been improved.

Effects on the Research Team

On this, LHJ limit their discussion to staffers' feelings about denying services to applicants. However, there were other problems in the research team as well. To a degree, these problems reflect the different logics of inquiry orienting outcome-oriented and process-oriented members of the team. They stemmed also from power relations within the team and from the penetration of all parts of the setting—including the research team itself—by participant–observers asking questions about things otherwise taken for granted by participants.

Where an intervention is failing or only marginally successful, the combination of experimental outcome measurement and intensive qualitative process evaluation is a recipe for conflict. In this case, tensions developed as qualitative researchers involved with the process evaluation effort began to conclude that the program staff had been unable to fully implement the intervention as planned, and also that the results of the intervention were weak at best. Whether and how these concerns should be interpreted and reported became points of contention within the project. As this comment demonstrates, these disagreements were not resolved within the research team.

Conclusion

This episode underscores the importance of attention to the effects of researcher involvement on social service programs. These effects may lead to unanticipated practical, ethical, and analytic problems, which may be obscured in the vision of participants by virtue of their own role in the setting under study. This suggests the importance of self-critical attention to these factors at every stage in the research process, from initial planning and project design, through problem-solving in project implementation, to final evaluation.

These developments also testify to the importance—and the difficulty—of combining process evaluation with outcome evaluation, and of attention to process issues within the research team required by such collaboration (Rossi and Wright, 1984). Ideally, research team leadership should have a grasp of *both* these logics of inquiry (as this team did on the outset of the research process). Outcome-oriented researchers must understand that case studies and ethnography are not employed mainly to provide illustrative quotes to "juice-up" evaluation reports, but rather can identify important factors that may be obscured in the experimental design. Otherwise, adding a qualitative component that is limited to gathering illustrative quotes from clients is likely to increase rather than decrease the danger of "malpractice in evaluation research" (Lipsey, 1988).

References

Hser, Y., Anglin, M. D., and Chou, O. P. "Evaluation of Drug Abuse Treatment: A Repeated Measures Design Assessing Methadone Maintenance." *Evaluation Review*, 1988, *12*, 547–70.

Leaf, P. J., and Thompson, K. "Research on Services for Homeless Substance Abusers." 1990 proposal to U.S. Department of Health and Human Services for funding for New Haven's Grant Street project.

Lipsey, M. "Practice and Malpractice in Evaluation Research." *Evaluation Practice,* 1988, *9* (4), 5–24.

Mesch, B., and Kandel, D. "Underreporting of Substance Use in a National Longitudinal Youth Cohort: Individual and Interviewer Effects." *Public Opinion Quarterly,* 1988, *52* (1), 100–124.

Rossi, P., and Wright, J. "Evaluation Research: An Assessment." *Annual Review of Sociology,* 1984.

PAUL JOHNSTON is an assistant professor in the Department of Sociology at Yale University.

PATRICK SWIFT is a graduate student in the Department of Sociology at Yale University.

They were members of the research team for the project discussed in Chapter Five.

Randomized experiments often fail for entirely avoidable reasons. Drawing on examples from the NIAAA Cooperative Agreement program and related literature, the authors present some tools and opportunities for using randomized designs more judiciously.

Judicious Application of Randomized Designs

Robert G. Orwin, David S. Cordray, Robert B. Huebner

In September 1990, the National Institute on Alcohol Abuse and Alcoholism (NIAAA) awarded funds to fourteen project sites under the Cooperative Agreements for Research Demonstration Projects on Alcohol and Other Drug Abuse Treatment for Homeless Persons (known as the Cooperative Agreement program). The authors served as national evaluators for the Cooperative Agreement program, several of whose investigators contributed chapters to this volume (see Cordray and others, 1991, for a detailed description of the national evaluation design). Our principal activity vis à vis the implementation and maintenance of grantees' evaluation designs was to provide monitoring and technical assistance. This was accomplished through a number of avenues including site visits, regular (bimonthly) and ad hoc phone contacts, semiannual gatherings of project teams, sponsorship of technical seminars, and data monitoring. The rationale underlying this form of proactive assistance was to identify and correct problems before they had a chance to seriously degrade the integrity of the evaluations.

Although the Cooperative Agreement was structured from the outset to encourage high quality evaluation designs, random assignment was not a requirement. Cognizant that a randomized test might not be appropriate or feasible in all cases, and not wishing to discourage good quasi-experimental alternatives, the request for applications (RFA) required only that "projects are expected to use the most rigorous research design(s) possible (that is, experimental and quasi-experimental designs)" (National Institute on Alcohol Abuse and Alcoholism and National Institute on Drug Abuse, 1990, p. 9). Although most of the fourteen funded proposals included random assignment to all groups, several did not. One was entirely nonrandom (though arguably "random-like"), and three others coupled randomized with nonrandomized designs. Two more added nonequivalent comparison groups later, with encouragement and technical assistance from NIAAA. Three of the remaining eight suspended randomization for certain time periods or subgroups to meet programmatic needs (for example, to keep facilities operating at capacity), so only five projects actually assigned all clients randomly. Applicants were also encouraged to supplement their experimental designs with more qualitative approaches (such as ethnographic studies).

As the national evaluators, we worked with each of the fourteen project teams as they wrestled with the challenges of implementing their designs. In this chapter, we try to capture some lessons from that experience about the judicious application of randomized experiments.

Tools for the Judicious Experimenter

In this section, we discuss some tools for improving the odds that an experiment will succeed: pipeline studies, pilot tests of the randomization, centralized control of randomization, broadened participation in the design, and implementation monitoring. We draw examples from prior literature on experimentation as well as the experience of the Cooperative Agreement program. The discussion assumes a prior determination that the experiment will answer an important question and can be designed to meet good ethical standards.

Pipeline Studies. A pipeline study is a formal assessment of client flow. It typically focuses on the points of entry of clients into the system and the points at which constriction of flow occur (Boruch, Riess, Larntz, and Garner, 1990). Such a study can answer a number of useful questions, such as what proportion of the qualifying population will actually be identified and selected as eligible and willing to participate, and how and where in the pipeline cases are excluded. It is generally necessary to assess whether target sample sizes can realistically be achieved, particularly in substance abuse treatment trials (Ashery and McAuliffe, 1992). The need for pipeline studies has long been recognized, but they are only infrequently conducted. Numerous experiments have been seriously undermined as a result (see Bickman, 1985).

In the Cooperative Agreement, projects were responsible for their own estimates of client flow as part of the application process. Some proposals contained excellent pipeline analyses that projected client flow quite accurately. Others contained thorough analyses, but the projected flow did not materialize due to operational weaknesses in follow-through with referral sources. Still others were simply unconvincing. We got involved primarily when the expected flow did not materialize.

For example, one project proposed a randomized comparison of a residential and nonresidential intervention, supplemented by a nonequivalent "usual services" comparison group. Based on the first seven months of operation, it appeared that if the recruitment remained consistent with the early experiences, the project would enroll less than 60 percent of its target sample size. Although there were several "feeder agencies," it was clear from the referral patterns that nearly 80 percent of the referrals had come from only three general sources, and the month-to-month figures were erratic for each. In addition, the nonequivalent comparison group had not been formed. We met with staff at four promising referral agencies to obtain estimates of the number of potential referrals to the program, as well as the number of agency clients who might be interested in participating in the research only. These individuals could form the nonequivalent comparison group.

From information gathered during interviews with staff at each referral site, we derived estimates of potential flow. During each interview, we tried to obtain a rough idea of the daily census of clients, the average length of stay and turnover, estimates of the number of clients who might be eligible for the project, estimates of the fraction of eligible clients who might be interested in participating in the program, provided that they would be willing to be randomly assigned, and estimates of the number who would be eligible for the program but willing to be only in the research part of the study. In an effort to derive a realistic estimate of the number of individuals who might actually participate in the program or the comparison group, the final monthly counts were adjusted downward to reflect a 70 percent participation rate (this assumed that all referral sources and groups would have the same agreement rates). Based on agreement rates derived from other projects, 70 percent appeared to be conservative. Because referral agencies generally do not have precise counts of the number of clients who may be eligible and because the nature of the site influences turnover (clients referred from jails have lower turnover rates than from shelters, for example), it is difficult to obtain firm information on potential client flow from each referral source. Thus, it is critical to ask very specific questions of referral agency staff about any estimated numbers they provide. Considerable leakage can occur between the estimated number of potential eligibles and the actual number of true eligibles (in our case, homeless with a substance abuse problem) who are successfully contacted, screened, agree to participate, assigned, and show up for treatment.

Under reasonably conservative assumptions, we concluded that these four referral sources could produce forty-eight new clients per month for the interventions and thirty-six clients per month for the comparison group. Given the number of clients proposed for each group in the initial application, the amount of time remaining in the project timeline for recruiting, the capacity and duration of the program, and estimated retention levels, we estimated that even if the project staff focused only on the four referral sites that were visited, client flow would be sufficient to meet the recruitment target. Recognizing that individuals who are interested only in the comparison group are likely to differ from those who agree to be randomized to an intervention, we also encouraged (in this site and others where a nonequivalent group was added midstream) that the core assessment battery be augmented with measures for modeling the selection process. Among Cooperative Agreement projects, it was generally agreed that the principal difference between eligible clients who agreed to participate and those who did not was their motivation and readiness for treatment. Consequently, a scale for assessing this was adopted at several sites.

Given the pattern of referrals relative to the analysis of potential referrals, it appeared that despite some early efforts by the project team, the program and the research staff at this site had not established or maintained sufficient relationships with the most promising referral agencies. A number of steps were taken to rectify the problems, such as solidifying responsibility for implementing the recruitment plan, developing a working relationship with the referral sources, and establishing recruitment goals for each referral site. The results were as hoped: Referrals increased and recruitment targets were largely met.

At a second project, a similar analysis revealed that even with projected improvements in client flow, there would not be time to run sufficient numbers of clients through the interventions to meet the sample size target. We therefore searched for other possible solutions and identified three: (1) lengthen the evaluation period, (2) increase the capacity of the intervention, and (3) reduce the duration of the intervention. Solution 1 was not feasible, even with a no-cost extension, and Solution 2 was not feasible because the intervention was housed in a residential facility with a finite number of beds. Solution 3, however, appeared viable. After discussions with research and program staff, the consensus was that the originally proposed treatment of six months could be intensified and reduced to four months with no predicted loss of efficacy. This made meeting the target far more likely. We need to emphasize that when considering a solution that actually changes the intervention, such as this one, it is critical to ensure that all research and program players accept it. If the change disrupts or dilutes the test of the intervention from a program theory standpoint, or if the program managers and staff do not fully support it, increased sample size may be a Pyrrhic victory. The experimenter runs the risk of protecting internal validity at the expense of other types, as discussed by Conrad and Conrad (this volume). A pipeline study can also address some of the generalizability issues raised earlier in this volume (in Stevens, for example), such as the degree to which eligible persons declined participation because of randomization (see Collins and Elkin, 1985).

Pilot Tests of the Randomization. It is both common practice and common sense to pilot test a new intervention before subjecting it to an outcome evaluation. Pilot tests of the randomization protocol are far less common yet no less commonsensical. The entire sequence of procedures—from the agencies referring clients to the study, the clients being approached and interviewed, the research staff doing the randomizing, and the service providers receiving clients after their assignments—should be piloted as realistically as possible to identify potential problems such as low acceptance rates.

There was no requirement to pilot the randomization procedures of the Cooperative Agreement projects, and several procedures had to be modified after startup due to unanticipated conflicts in the field. In one case, the initial procedure had the sealed envelope that contained the assignment on display during the baseline interview. The rat ionale seemed sensible: Provide physical proof to skeptical clients that their responses could not affect their assignment, thereby engendering greater candor about alcohol/drug use, criminal history, and so on. When implemented, however, the procedure created a game-show environment in which clients tried to race through the interview to find out what was inside the envelope. In this case, a procedure designed to reduce response distortion was actually increasing it.

A second problem arose because clients had to wait at the detox unit after being assigned, sometimes for days, while paperwork was processed for their residential placement. This gave the detox staff, who had worked with the clients and formed their own opinions about appropriate care for each one (and disliked the randomization to boot), the opportunity to negatively bias clients before they even began. In the revised procedures, the displayed envelopes were scrapped and clients were transported to their placement immediately after assignment. Had the randomization been piloted, the revised procedures would have been in place before the main study began.

Assuming that the experiment includes a pretest or some sort of baseline data collection, a pilot test of the randomization can also provide early warning of problems with the randomization itself and determine whether it is actually creating equivalent groups. In monitoring the early baseline data from the Cooperative Agreement projects, we found that some of the randomization schemes were yielding nonequivalences beyond chance expectations. Because there was no pilot, however, most of the target sample size had already been assigned by the time this was detected. Diagnostic analyses of pilot data are typically limited by the small sample sizes, but they can at least identify patterns to watch for once the main study begins.

Centralized Control of Randomization Procedures. Conner (1977) first demonstrated the association between centralized researcher control and success of randomization, and the theme has been reiterated numerous times since (Gueron, 1985). Boruch and Wothke (1985) cite some famous failures caused in part by lack of such controls. The chosen mechanism for exercising control will vary with the scope and intent of the experiment, but the basic guidelines are as follows:

Whatever the randomization procedure, the researchers should maintain control of it at all times.
Keep it simple. The more people involved, the more chance for something to go awry.
Think through how the proposed procedure can be undermined, either intentionally or inadvertently, and take steps to protect it.

Try to prevent "unhappy" randomization, that is, the advent of group non-equivalence by chance (for example, by stratifying on variables of concern before assignment).

The guidelines may be old hat to veteran experimenters, but they are not always followed in the field, and were not always followed in the Cooperative Agreement. In an earlier version of their article, Lam, Hartwell, and Jekel (this volume) described the pressures on the individual responsible for drawing the numbers being lobbied by clients, family members, and staff to let a particular client into the experimental group. "Many times I have found myself sitting there looking at the list of random numbers, thinking about the power I have over their lives." Clearly, the basic guidelines would preclude selecting such a vulnerable procedure. If a person must be in the loop, then it is best if that person have no familiarity with clients or the clinical work of the project. Technology can help. Braucht and Reichardt (1993) developed and implemented a nearly foolproof computerized trickle-process randomization procedure for their evaluation of a case management program. It included encryption of all data files containing assignment information, thereby minimizing the vulnerability to corruption.

Broadened Participation in the Design. Central control of the randomization procedures protects the assignment process, but assignment is only one of many points at which randomized designs can be undermined. Control wanes once the client is exposed to the intervention; new people are in the loop and their attitudes toward the experiment may be less than sympathetic.

The judicious planning of experiments should, therefore, include attention to the natural concerns of service providers. Social scientists' anxieties over evidence are not uppermost among them, at least when weighed against denying a "valuable" treatment component to any group of desperately needy clients. The case that efforts to circumvent random assignment are ethically misguided when effectiveness is unknown (Boruch, 1976) should be presented to frontline providers and program administrators and reiterated as implementation difficulties and staff turnover raise the issue again. But the arguments may not persuade line staff who already "know" the treatment "works," and are deeply—even zealously—committed to the population. This may be particularly true of case managers, a key component in thirteen of the fourteen Cooperative Agreement projects (Cordray and others, 1991). By selection, training, and characteristic ideology, case managers can be more determined and effective than other program staff in circumventing "bureaucratic" rules that obstruct the delivery of services to clients (Frederickson, 1993). Some will see random assignment as just another rule they need to circumvent. As noted by Boruch and Wothke (1985), just because opponents have been silenced does not mean they have been persuaded.

It is therefore important to incorporate input from case managers and other providers, as well as from program directors and supervisors, into the design of the experiment, as other authors in this volume have also suggested. Consideration should also be given to providing the services considered most crucial by service providers (such as housing if clients are homeless) to all study participants whenever feasible, with randomized comparisons being reserved for other components. Gathering empirical data on clients' reactions to their assignment can also be helpful. Lam, Hartwell, and Jekel, (this volume) found large variation in the response of clients assigned to the control group. Some expressed the expected resentment, but others were philosophical or said flatly that they had no desire to enter the experimental program; they only wanted the quick detox that participants in both groups received. Service providers, on the other hand, perceived far more demoralization among control group clients than actually existed. Conveying such data to those providers may reduce their negativity toward the experiment.

Sensitivity to staff burden will also help garner support because most social service staff are overworked enough without having new requirements imposed on them. Gueron (1985) describes how she carefully constructed procedures so that all paperwork and phone calling by line staff was limited to fifteen minutes per client. Effects on the organizational climate should also be considered. The introduction of an experiment into an existing organization is an event of major change that must be "managed." Failure to communicate properly with all staff members could result in alienation and sabotage.

The potential impact of random assignment on referral agencies (discussed in this volume by Lam, Hartwell, and Jekel and by Stevens) is also important because those agencies can undermine client flow. This can limit generalizability as well as power. Lam, Hartwell, and Jekel describe how the attitude of the referral agencies toward the research study can be improved through accommodations from the research staff that do not compromise the randomization. In that experiment, the perception of improved relationships was supported by a measurable increase in the referral rate.

Finally, gaining the support of service providers is necessary but not sufficient. It may keep them from intentionally undermining the experiment, but not from doing so inadvertently. They should also be given a clear explanation of the importance of the procedures, what they should and should not do or say, and so forth. Even then, the experimenter must be aware that explaining the randomization does not guarantee that it will be understood. In a multisite test of school improvement incentives, Bickman (1985) asked principals two questions: Will all participating schools have an even chance of being selected into the incentive group? and Is there a way to enhance your school's chance of being selected? Although the randomization procedure had been explained in numerous meetings and memoranda, only 60 percent of the principals answered both questions correctly.

Implementation Monitoring. Too many experiments fail because the experimental conditions are more similar as implemented than as proposed. The intent of the judicious experimenter is not to artificially bolster ineffective interventions, but rather to ensure that all interventions are tested with fairness, fidelity to the program theory, and sufficient sensitivity for the effective ones to be detected. In monitoring the implementation of the Cooperative Agreement projects, we observed a number of ways in which distinctions between groups were being muddied. About six months into implementation, we tallied them up. The summary results are shown in Table 7.1. Contamination or leakage was the most common threat, potentially blurring the distinction between groups in more than half the projects.

When these threats arise in the field, they should be addressed. Often the solution is quite simple. One of the Cooperative Agreement projects compared an intensive residential program with supportive services to a usual care condition. As this project was implemented, two concerns were raised. First, it appeared that the usual services offered by the community were beginning to approximate the service activities offered in the experimental group. Apart from narrowing the difference between intervention groups, continual change in the wider community's service delivery system was making it difficult to describe the services received by usual care clients. Second, it was discovered that some program staff were active in efforts to change the local service delivery system, serving as social activists to improve usual services. With the best of intentions, therefore, they were undermining the experiment from within.

A number of steps were taken once these issues were identified and discussed. First, the social activism was curtailed. The changing delivery system was not controllable, but efforts were made to document the changes that did occur as extensively as possible. In principle, this permits them to be taken into account at the analysis phase. Regarding further augmentations to the usual services condition, we met with city officials and stressed the need to be sure that the treatment group received access to the same services. Both city representatives and project staff understood the importance of maintaining group comparability on non-project-related resources.

In a second project, the issue of *crossovers* arose, that is, clients who were assigned to one condition but effectively received components of another. The project compared three conditions: supervised housing and case management integrated with alcohol and drug treatment and vocational and educational services (Group 1); monitored shelter and intensive case management with a community network of services (Group 2); and typical shelter services with usual casework (Group 3). It was discovered that some clients from Groups 2 and 3 had been referred to the Group 1 residence, and that some Group 3 clients had access to some Group 2 services because the two groups were housed in the same building. In part, the crossovers were due to inadequate administrative controls, but they also reflected a tradition at the service agency of encouraging clients' initiative to improve their situation, which potentially conflicted with the experimental design.

After some discussion, the administrative controls were strengthened to prevent erroneous referrals and the project team agreed to "flag" the crossovers,

Table 7.1. Threats to Distinctions Between Intervention Groups in Cooperative Agreement Projects

Threat	Description	Affected Projects
Similarity of "active ingredient"	When an ingredient common to each group potentially overwhelms other distinctions (for example, when a strict relapse policy applied to all groups has a greater influence on criterion-relevant behavior than do differences in service packages).	4
Upgrade of usual care	When the implementation of an experimental design in an existing service organization triggers the improvement of usual services to the control group. Alternatively, usual care can improve for reasons independent of the experiment (such as an infusion of new services into the locality).	6
Contamination or leakage	Unintended diffusion of intervention components across groups, such as might occur when multiple groups are housed in the same facility or when a single set of case managers are expected to provide differing service levels to different groups. Can also reflect crossovers—clients pursuing or receiving the service package associated with a group other that to which they were assigned.	8
Dilution of intervention	The delivery of an intervention in a weaker dose than that proposed. Can occur at the point of delivery or receipt, and generally results from implementation and startup problems.	4
Insensitivity of sample to intervention	Typically reflects one of two extremes: *creaming,* (restricting the sample to a highly functioning, highly motivated subgroup that may do well regardless of which intervention they receive); or *dredging,* (restricting it to low-functioning clients who may not be capable of detectable improvements in the brief intervention period, such as dully diagnosed clients).	6
Lack of usual care comparison base	When a project has multiple interventions, each potentially effective, but no comparison base that represents how the clients would have done in the absence of these interventions (such as a usual services or control group). The interventions are likely to perform similarly, and their differential effect is difficult to demonstrate unequivocally.	4

to assess the extent of the problem, and to permit identification of those individuals in the analysis. As a result, covering all possible combinations, crossovers occurred in only 3 percent of the sample. The example suggests a two-pronged approach for the judicious experimenter: Try to prevent the threat and assess how well it was prevented. A threat ruled out is no longer a threat.

Sometimes stronger action is warranted, including a modification to the basic design. A third project initially attempted to implement a 2 x 2 factorial comparison of on-site case management and vocational training services. The design created enormous constraints on program operations. The staff was vigilant in keeping the four groups apart, but this was significantly complicated by the fact that all clients resided in one transitional shelter that was too small to provide separate living quarters for each group. To cope, program staff established rules and scheduling constraints that limited clients' activities and movement as well as their referral to community services. The structure was viewed as arbitrary and unrealistic by clients. Moreover, there was little observable difference between the experimental and comparison interventions.

Many of these problems stemmed from the fact that the project was too complex. Rather than using a fully crossed factorial design, we recommended that the project contrast just two groups—on-site case management plus prevocational services versus usual-care case management and training opportunities. By reducing the number of conditions, problems associated with scheduling activities could be reduced, more tailored attention could be provided to the "high-intensity condition," caseloads in the groups could be reduced, and the floor plan could be altered to optimize recovery activities. The design change did not solve all the project's problems, but it increased the possibility that groups would differ as intended and the experiment would remain viable. Of course, with the loss of the factorial design, the separate effects of case management and vocational train ing could no longer be isolated. It was becoming obvious, however, that design simplification was necessary to salvage the study. The new design, though less elegant, could work. If it did, it would make a worthwhile contribution to the literature. Experimentation is a gamble, and judicious experimenters must know when to cut their losses.

Opportunities for Improvement

It has been noted that we know less than we should about designing experiments (Boruch and Wothke, 1985). If our experience is any indication, then we also use less than we know. Consequently, more experiments fail than should.

For example, we sometimes read requests for proposals (RFPs) that specify the use of randomization with little regard to adequacy of time, money, incentives, administrative structure, and so on—in short, lacking most characteristics that thirty years of case experience has shown to be necessary for success. Education would help, no doubt, but we suspect that what we are reading reflects the unhappy or even cynical compromise of competing stakeholders (for example, the evaluator will implement a rigorous outcome design, but provision of outcome data will be voluntary so as to minimize grantee burden) as much as it does ignorance about mounting field experiments.

As shown by the NIAAA Cooperative Agreement, it does not have to be this way. There are many opportunities for the federal sponsor of multisite demonstrations to improve the likelihood that funded experiments can be successfully implemented. The structure of the Cooperative Agreement provided many of these opportunities, but future demonstrations could provide still more. They are present at all stages in the typical grant award and process—development of the RFA, preaward technical review, and postaward monitoring.

Development of the RFA. An encouraging trend in many RFAs is the emphasis on basic methodological requirements such as adequate sample sizes, comparative research designs, and use of reliable and valid measures. However, these requirements typically ignore many of the feasibility considerations for conducting a randomized study discussed in the previous section. Including these considerations in the requirements will not guarantee that applicants will be more judicious in their research design, but do send a clear message: Feasibility issues should not take a back seat to technical merit and methodological elegance in the design of a field experiment.

The primary purpose of the Cooperative Agreement (like other demonstration programs) was to demonstrate, not generalize. This does not preclude that features that promote generalizability be written into the requirements as well.

Pre-Award Technical Review. Although the review of an application's technical merit is typically conducted by an external review committee of nonfederal experts, federal staff do have two opportunities for input. First, they are resources on matters regarding agency intent and provide formal instructions on the program's priorities. Here, federal staff could proactively communicate the importance of considering feasibility issues in the proposed experiments under review. Funders and reviewers alike must recognize that if the RFA emphasizes strong evaluation designs, they will receive proposals for which a randomized design was, for all practical purposes, a device to increase the attractiveness of the proposal. Peer review groups need to ascertain whether investigators are committed to the design, have thought through its feasibility, have experience in implementing and maintaining experiments, and have included a fallback design so that all will not be lost if the randomization goes awry. The single most judicious thing an experimenter can do is plan for the experiment's failure.

Second, program staff can conduct preaward site visits to projects that receive favorable recommendations from the review committee. The current mandate for preaward site visits is quite limited; typically, applicants can be evaluated only on the adequacy of the project's organization, management, and physical plant. This type of preaward site visit was used in the Cooperative Agreement. Feasibility issues of the type described in this chapter were discussed, but most were officially off-limits as far as influencing the funding decision. The rationale was that it would be seen as second-guessing, and therefore threatening the independence of, the peer review process. Yet many of the implementation problems that did subsequently occur (including some of those described above) occurred essentially as predicted by the site visitors.

An expansion of this preaward site visit mandate to include feasibility criteria would significantly increase the probability that projects eventually selected for funding could successfully implement their experimental designs. At a minimum, the site visitors should interview investigators (including statisticians), service providers, community representatives, and prospective clients, and should also examine data relevant to client flow and the local system of care. A pipeline study could be incorporated into the visit if the proposal did not include a convincing one. Proper coordination with the external review committee would ensure preservation of the integrity and independence of peer review.

Postaward Monitoring. The technical assistance component of postaward monitoring is usually grantee-driven. Grantees conduct needs assessments of their research operations and contact the funding agency for technical assistance in meeting those needs. As described earlier, technical assistance can also be provided proactively, and both varieties were provided in the Cooperative Agreement program. Our experience suggested that proactive technical assistance can significantly increase the odds of an experiment succeeding.

Postaward monitoring also includes the funding renewal decision after the first year award. There are two approaches to continuation funding: competitive and noncompetitive. In the former, a project must respond to a second RFA and undergo a technical review by the external review committee. In the latter, it submits a brief renewal application, and review is conducted by in-house federal staff. The competitive approach offers the best opportunity to leverage full compliance with the approved research design, but is costly in terms of time and human resources. The noncompetitive approach, which is less costly but provides less leverage, could be strengthened. Experiments fail despite the best intentions, so it would not be appropriate to withhold or threaten to withhold funding simply because the design went sour. However, if the grantee resisted offers of technical assistance or refused to implement a suitable fallback design, termination would be justified. Experiments are expensive, so failed experiments are expensive failures.

Problem Experiments in Perspective

Several chapters in this volume have discussed the very real problems that arise in carrying out social experiments. We do not wish to minimize the logistical and ethical difficulties associated with implementing field experiments or the struggles faced by the project investigators in making them work. Finding ways to make them work was our goal as well.

Some perspective is in order, however. No one who has studied the history of social experimentation could realistically expect trouble-free success in all fourteen projects, particularly considering the target population. Although social experimentation is no longer in its infancy, its application to programs for homeless persons with substance abuse problems or mental illness is. The experiments that predated the Cooperative Agreement were few (Orwin, Sonnefeld, Garrison-Mogren, and Smith, 1994). Moreover, homeless substance-abusing clients do pose special methodological problems that make the already difficult task of mounting a field experiment more difficult still (Huebner and Crosse, 1991).

Although some projects did experience obstacles in maintaining their randomized designs, several others went quite smoothly. This merits mention here because those projects were not discussed in this volume. They met their recruitment targets, successfully implemented their randomization procedures, retained clients in treatment, maintained clear distinctions between experimental conditions, and posted an adequate follow-up rate in all groups. Nothing in their screening procedures limited generalizability in any obvious way.

Finally, our own national evaluation plan (written before implementation) explicitly recognized design degradation as a fact of evaluation life. In addition to the proactive technical assistance to prevent or at least limit the degradation in the field, the plan instituted data systems that monitor the degradation and enable it to be incorporated and modeled in the analysis of outcomes (Cordray and others, 1991). We make no claim that our modeling efforts will fully compensate for the degradation, as the state of the science does not yet warrant such claims, but we remain optimistic that all projects (short of one that was terminated early) will ultimately yield interpretable results.

Randomized designs can and do frequently succeed, and will succeed more often if applied more judiciously. A thoughtfully designed experiment remains the best hope for unambiguous causal inferences about program effectiveness. The policy maker, who must choose how to allocate scarce resources, should expect and demand no less than rigorous, unequivocal evidence to guide that choice. This is particularly the case for evaluations involving the at-risk populations discussed in this volume, where the stakes can quite literally be life or death.

References

Ashery, R. S., and McAuliffe, W. E. "Implementation Issues and Techniques in Randomized Trials of Outpatient Psychosocial Treatments for Drug Abusers: Recruitment of Subjects." *American Journal of Drug and Alcohol Abuse,* 1992, *18,* 305–29.

Bickman, L. "Randomized Field Experiments in Education: Implementation Lessons." In R. F. Boruch and W. Wothke (eds.), *Randomization and Field Experimentation.* New Directions for Program Evaluation, no. 28. San Francisco: Jossey-Bass, 1985.

Boruch, R. F. "On Common Contentions about Randomized Field Experiments." In R. F. Boruch and H. W. Riecken (eds.), *Experimental Tests of Public Policy*. Boulder, Colo.: Westview Press, 1976.

Boruch, R. F., Riess, A., Larntz, K., and Garner, J. "Learning What Works Better: Some Guidelines on Randomized Experiments." Paper presented at the National Institute of Justice Seminar on Experimental Design and Urine Testing and Treatment, Washington, D.C., June 20, 1990.

Boruch, R. F., and Wothke, W. "Seven Kinds of Randomization Plans for Designing Field Experiments." In R. F. Boruch and W. Wothke (eds.), *Randomization and Field Experimentation*. New Directions for Program Evaluation, no. 28. San Francisco: Jossey-Bass, 1985.

Braucht, N. G., and Reichardt, C. S. "A Computerized Approach to Trickle-Process, Random Assignment." *Evaluation Review*, 1993, *17*, 79–90.

Collins, J. F., and Elkin, I. "Randomization in the NIMH Treatment of Depression Collaborative Research Program." In R. F. Boruch and W. Wothke (eds.), *Randomization and Field Experimentation*. New Directions for Program Evaluation, no. 28. San Francisco: Jossey-Bass, 1985.

Conner, R. F. "Selecting a Control Group: An Analysis of the Randomization Process in Twelve Social Reform Programs." *Evaluation Quarterly*, 1977, *1*, 195–244.

Cordray, D. S., and others. *Final National Evaluation Plan*. Rockville, Md.: R.O.W. Sciences, Inc. and Vanderbilt Institute for Public Policy Studies for the National Institute on Alcohol Abuse and Alcoholism, 1991.

Frederickson, A. "Denver Cooperative Agreement Project Presentation." Presented to the Working Group Meeting of the NIAAA Cooperative Agreements for Research Demonstration Projects on Alcohol and Other Drug Abuse Treatments for Homeless Persons, Washington, D.C., March 4, 1993.

Gueron, J. M. "The Demonstration of State Work/Welfare Initiatives." In R. F. Boruch and W. Wothke (eds.), *Randomization and Field Experimentation*. New Directions for Program Evaluation, no. 28. San Francisco: Jossey-Bass, 1985.

Huebner, R. B., and Crosse, S. B. "Challenges in Evaluating a National Demonstration Program for Homeless Persons with Alcohol and other Drug Problems." In D. J. Rog (ed.), *Evaluating Programs for the Homeless*. New Directions for Program Evaluation, no. 52. San Francisco: Jossey-Bass, 1991.

National Institute on Alcohol Abuse and Alcoholism and National Institute on Drug Abuse. *Cooperative Agreements for Research Demonstration Projects on Alcohol and Other Drug Abuse Treatment for Homeless Persons* (RFA AA-90–01). Rockville, Md.: U.S. Department of Health and Human Services, Jan. 1990.

Orwin, R. G., Sonnefeld, L. J., Garrison-Mogren, R., and Smith, N. G. "Pitfalls in Evaluating the Effectiveness of Case Management Programs for Homeless Persons: Lessons from the NIAAA Community Demonstration Program." *Evaluation Review*, 1994, *18* (2), 153–207.

ROBERT G. ORWIN is research director at R.O.W. Sciences, Inc., a health sciences and professional services firm in Rockville, Md.

DAVID S. CORDRAY is professor of public policy and psychology and chair of the Department of Human Resources at Vanderbilt University.

ROBERT B. HUEBNER is acting chief of the Homeless Demonstration and Evaluation Branch, National Institute on Alcohol Abuse and Alcoholism.

*Most evaluators of social programs have little training or experi-
ence in designing or conducting field experiments. The goal of this
chapter is to describe strategies that could be used to improve the
design, implementation, and analysis of randomized field experiments.*

Improving the Quality of
Randomized Field Experiments:
Tricks of the Trade

Michael L. Dennis, Robert F. Boruch

Randomized field experiments have been used to evaluate social policy and
programs for more than sixty years and have been partially responsible for
major changes in a wide range of areas. Numerous reviews have already been
written establishing that these experiments have been successfully conducted
in a variety of substantive areas (Rieken, and others, 1974), programs (Berk
and others, 1985), and countries (Dennis and Boruch, 1989). Several studies
have also been published on the threshold conditions for deciding whether to
do an experiment (Dennis and Boruch, 1989; Federal Judicial Center, 1981),
how to design an experiment (Fairweather and Tornatzky, 1977; Fisher, 1960;
Lipsey, 1990; Saxe and Fine, 1981), how to assess an experiment's validity
(Campbell and Stanley, 1963; Cook and Campbell, 1979; Dennis, 1990), and
how to model the effects of multiple-dimension and multiple-exposure interventions (Bentler, 1991; Blalock, 1985; Dennis, Fairbank, and Rachal, 1992;
Efron and Feldman, 1991).

Although the use of randomized field experiments is not without its own
problems, this method still appears to be one of the best available ways to compare the relative effectiveness of two or more programs, regimens, or services.
Unfortunately, most evaluators have little training or personal experience in
designing or conducting field experiments. In a study of the major experiments

The authors thank Ken Conrad and the other reviewers for their thoughtful critiques. They
also thank Linda B. Parker, Bruce MacDonald, and Richard S. Straw for assistance in prepar-
ing the manuscript. This chapter was partially supported by grant #P50-DA06990 from the
National Institute on Drug Abuse.

funded by the National Institute of Justice (NIJ) over a fifteen-year period, Dennis (1988) found that only 7 percent of the experiments were based on pilot studies or earlier experiments and that for more than half of the evaluators this was their first experiment. As might be expected, many of these studies had more problems with their intervention and implementation than did those of more experienced investigators.

In earlier works, we have already discussed some of the common contentions about doing randomized field experiments (Boruch, 1976), the threshold conditions that should be met before conducting an experiment (Dennis and Boruch, 1989), assessments of their implementation and validity (Dennis, 1988, 1990), and how to design them (Boruch, 1987; Dennis, in press). The goal of this chapter is to identify some of the lesser known strategies that could be used to improve the quality of the design, implementation, and analysis of randomized field experiments.

Some Tricks of the Trade

Several tricks of the trade offer potential strategies for improving the quality of randomized field experiments. Although they may not always be feasible or appropriate for every study, they are often used by investigators who have conducted multiple field experiments. We have tried to clarify some of the key problems and to identify some of the strategies that can potentially be used to address them.

Design. In contrast to laboratory experiments, field experiments are typically longer (often by years), organizationally more complicated (involving multiple sites, organizations, and staff), and used to evaluate more complicated interventions (involving multiple components and multiple-exposure interventions). Furthermore, many try to incorporate more diversity in sites, staff, and clients in order to improve generalizability. These differences mean that randomized field experiments are relatively rare within any specific field, that few evaluators have experience in designing or implementing them, and that few evaluators go back to do a second experiment to take advantage of what they learned the first time. In the following sections, we summarize some of the strategies for improving the quality of the design for experiments.

STRATEGY 1. *Define a relevant experimental contrast and ask questions to draw out its implications.*

Perhaps the most important step is to clearly define what you are trying to accomplish with the intervention so that it can guide the research design. This means asking the following key questions:

What is the target population, and is this population different from the program's regular clients? How can these people and their needs be identified? What barriers currently prevent them from fully using the intervention or using it more effectively?

How can the proposed changes in the intervention address the needs of this group? What new components are needed? Does everyone need every component or service to the same extent or level?

How can the intervention be designed to accommodate the needs and desires of both the targeted clients and practitioners? How will the intervention be integrated into the existing service system? What resource gaps must be filled to make the intervention work in the existing system?

What changes is the intervention expected to produce? How soon will they occur? How large will they be? What secondary effects might they have?

Is the intervention or level of competing services likely to change during the experiment? Will more services be added? What is the expected rate of staff turnover? Are major programs starting up or ending in the community that may affect the main outcome measures?

What are the likely threats to the experiment's validity? Are clients or practitioners likely to refuse participation or resist some components? Are any of the components likely to produce experimental contamination or compensatory rivalry?

In a field setting, compensatory rivalry can take on many forms. On the one hand, an administrator may allocate more discretionary funds or services to the control group or program. On the other hand, an administrator may actively oppose the experiment. In a randomized field experiment of a community penalties program, for instance, Wallace (1987) found that lawyers in a district attorney's office thought that an experimental program was too pro-defense and refused to plea bargain with defendants in the experimental groups.

STRATEGY 2. *Minimize preinclusion attrition and plan measures to determine generalizability.*

Although randomization addresses issues involving internal validity or causal inference, it does nothing to address the issue of external validity or generalizability. Externality is often overlooked, but it is of great importance if we assume that field experiments are done, at least in part, to make the results more generalizable to practice. The implication is that we have to pay greater attention to identifying the target population to which the study will be generalized, carefully documenting who is screened out of the study and why, and using strategies such as random or stratified sampling to improve generalizability.

Consider, for instance, the experiment with disulfiram to treat alcoholism (by Fuller and others 1986). Of the 6,629 clients presenting for treatment at the 9 participating Veterans' Administration medical centers, 5,011 (76 percent) were screened out because of exclusionary criteria (that is, because they lived alone, had another medical condition, or lived more than 80 kilometers from the hospital), and 1,028 (62 percent of the eligible clients) refused to participate. It is unclear to whom the results of the remaining 602 clients (10 percent) can be generalized.

A related issue is to specifically identify and collect data that can be used to compare the programs, staff, and clients with the universe to which you wish to generalize. After representative sampling, the next best thing is to be able to describe what you have done in such a way that other people can judge how similar or dissimilar their situations are. Alcohol and drug treatment program directors, for instance, are required to describe their client population to the states for the National Drug and Alcoholism Treatment Unit Survey (NDA-TUS). By asking the same basic questions, other programs can judge which of several sites (or which overall study) is closest to their own situation.

STRATEGY 3. *Prioritize analysis plans and design decisions.*

Many randomized field experiments start with a laundry list of potential analyses. In addition to planning overall sample sizes, power analysis can help focus the analysis plan by identifying what can be done well, what can be done medium well, and what can be done only badly. Once this is determined, it can help to identify areas where ot her components may need to be strengthened to improve sensitivity. This might include blocking (that is, randomly assigning people within a subgroup) or using repeated measures. To the extent that there are almost always resource constraints, this process will also help to identify where to invest resources. See Dennis (1994) or Lipsey (1990) for a more detailed discussion of prioritizing plans and decisions.

Blocking also has the virtue of providing some insurance against partial failures. In conducting an experiment on whether women could bring their children with them to a therapeutic community, Renner and Sechrest (1992) experienced problems in obtaining compliance with assignment because some mothers did not want their children present and still others did not have legal custody of them. In hindsight, clients could have been classified before randomization into two levels of motivation by two custody classifications. Women within each of the four cells could then have been randomly assigned at the same ratio or ratios that varied by block (for example, to give more preference to women who wanted their children). This procedure would have ensured that the clients were equally distributed and would mean that if the experiment failed for one block (because of noncompliance or high attrition), the others could still be analyzed.

In general, methodological and treatment concerns should be given equal attention. Evaluators can become obsessed with potential methodological problems to the point that design decisions are made that create actual problems for the successful implementation of the intervention. Some situations in which an imbalance is likely to happen include the following:

*Limiting random assignment to programs out of fear that within-site random-
ization might cause contamination.* This decision may greatly reduce the generalizability of the findings and confound them with what may be large program
differences. Such differences may make it almost impossible to identify the key
components that produced any observed differences. One potential solution
is to collect baseline (pre- and post-) information on a group of people receiving the intervention before the experiment's implementation. Potential contamination can then be assessed by comparing the baseline and standard groups
(who are expected to exhibit the same trends) in a time series design.

Placing randomization too early in the treatment entry process. Although this
may improve generalizability, it can result in high intervention attrition (versus research attrition) and result in a very small difference between the experimental, standard, and control groups. If there is inherently high attrition rate,
such as in acquired immune deficiency syndrome (AIDS) outreach or drug-
free treatment, the experiment can be reconceptualized as a two or more stage
process with a new level of randomization for clients who reach each subsequent stage. It is important to realize that this approach is appropriate for a
multistage process and ensures that each phase has one or more key outcome
measures before the next stage.

To illustrate this strategy, consider the evaluation of an AIDS outreach to
injection drug users. If randomization occurs early in the recruitment process,
too many people may drop out before receiving the full educational part of the
intervention. One simple way to address such multistage interventions is to
develop a multistage design. In this case, outreach can be divided into its two
main components: (1) finding and recruiting appropriate people, and (2)
designing an intervention to encourage treatment and reduce risk. To test the
first component, geographical units can be randomly assigned to two different
approaches to outreach. To increase statistical power or sensitivity, random
assignment can be done within key types of geographical areas (counties, prior
outreach areas, public housing units, the remainder of the ZIP code). The main
outcomes for the first experiment could be the number of eligible people identified, their characteristics (the experimental group could target more women
and people under age thirty), and the number of people who actually show up
at the field station for the second component.

To test the second component, people showing up at the field station
could be rescreened for eligibility and randomly assigned to one of two interventions. To control for potential interactions, random assignment should be
statistically blocked on the type of recruitment in the first stage. To increase
statistical power, random assignment can also be blocked within key subgroups (for example, by gender or age). Here, the outcome measures are treatment entry, access to other services, and risk reduction.

Too many selection criteria. Although a long or extensive selection process
may reduce attrition and variability among subjects, it may also produce a
highly selective sample that no longer represents the people presenting for

treatment or those for whom the intervention is intended. In the preceding example, if we randomized only the people who came to the field station, we would not know about the effectiveness of the efforts to identify and recruit them. Again, it is important to consider to whom we hope to generalize data about the intervention's effectiveness. If the intervention does not reach enough people in appropriate strength, then it would be more appropriate to r evise the intervention than to simply push back the point of randomization. Pilot studies and experience in similar experiments can eventually help determine the balance between the placement of randomization and the intervention strength.

Failing to measure the actual amount of intervention provided to each group. Obviously, the experimental intervention should not be provided to the standard or control group, but it is necessary to measure whether randomization was ignored and an intervention actually was provided. As in all experiments, it is also essential to measure the extent to which similar interventions or services are being obtained by either group through other sources. The concept of a placebo or control group is often meaningless in field studies. Denying access to a service provider may actually be a negative condition if it results in the denial of access to services that had previously been available. It is therefore more appropriate to think of the nonexperimental groups as standard or comparison groups who are receiving something—something that needs to be measured.

Dividing clinically necessary teams or processes. In defining the intervention, it is essential to identify the treatment process and necessary components. Just as it would be imprudent to prevent a surgeon from using both hands, dividing a clinical team or key process may sabotage the intervention. Ideally, such clinical teams should be divided (and randomly assigned) into experimental or standard approaches. When this is not possible, concerns about potential contamination can be addressed using secondary data analysis such as time series analysis with a baseline group.

A special problem arises when the clinically relevant team also becomes the unit of random assignment for the study's subjects. This happens when randomly assigning schools, classrooms, group quarters, roommates, siblings, or married couples. Traditionally, the unit of random assignment is the same as the unit of analysis. In this case, however, an increasingly common approach is to adjust for the cluster variance at the group level and analyze the data as though individuals were randomly assigned (Donner, Birkett, and Buck, 1981; Donner and Donald, 1987). Depending on the size of the intraclass correlation, this approach produces an effective sample somewhere between the number of groups and the number of individuals. Based on sampling theory, it is essentially treating the unit of randomization as a primary sampling unit and correcting for the intraclass correlation with such software as SUrvey DAta ANalysis, or SUDAAN (Research Triangle Institute [RTI], 1991).

Preventing the intervention from changing in response to preliminary analysis or opportunities in the environment. Programs, like individuals, are dynamic and need to grow. Forcing them to remain stable over a long period of time is like restraining an individual. The result may be counterproductive. To the extent that programs normally adapt to funding and other environmental constraints, holding the program constant may also reduce the generalizability of the findings. Finally, failure to change the intervention in response to preliminary analysis or real changes in the environment may also reduce the likelihood of the intervention's success.

STRATEGY 4. *Maximize the design sensitivity.*

Assuming that we have wisely chosen a meaningful improvement to test, several technical steps can still be taken to improve the design sensitivity and reduce the sample size requirements:

Increase the number of observations per person. Although there is a diminishing rate of return, repeated observations can reduce the required sample size fivefold or more. For instance, a pretest measure that is correlated .50 or more with later outcome measures will improve statistical power for normally distributed data (for example, pre- and post-measures of drug use or employment). (Also, see Strategy 6 on reducing attrition.)

Increase the number of people by collaborating across sites. It is almost impossible to study such subgroups as women or minorities without obtaining much larger samples. The simplest way to do this for most programs is to collaborate with other programs and use similar instruments, procedures, and interventions. The downside to this approach is that multiple sites become exponentially more difficult to manage.

Use blocking for both insurance and sensitivity. Residents should be categorized into meaningful subgroups before random assignment to ensure that the subgroups (not just the total number) are distributed as evenly as possible. In an experiment on vocational training, for instance, we blocked on gender, vocational readiness, and whether the person volunteered or was sampled randomly (Dennis and others, 1993). Because blocking has a diminishing return, it is generally beneficial only to do it on two to three key covariates.

Measure implementation and context. No findings can be meaningfully interpreted if we do not know whether the intervention was actually implemented at all, the extent to which it was implemented as planned, and the extent to which the amount of intervention received was related to random assignment. Failure to find a difference because the experimental intervention was never implemented is hardly a fair test of its effectiveness.

All of these strategies go back to how well-defined the intervention, expected effects, and planned analyses are. To the extent that subgroup analyses are planned, for instance, blocking should be considered either to ensure balanced sample sizes within analysis subgroups or to make the allocation of resources fairer or more logistically sound. Each component of the intervention should have corresponding implementation checks and outcome measures identified in advance. One problem in many experiments is the failure to obtain a baseline measure of functioning or services received during the pretest. A related issue is when the measure or instrumentation changes between the pre- and posttest. To the extent possible, the instrumentation should be as stable as possible. (See Cook and Campbell, 1979, for a more detailed discussion of the threats to instrumentation validity.)

Implementation. Although a well-planned design is important, field experiments also require good management and quality control. The evaluator also has to anticipate the unexpected. This means watching for anomalies and potential problems and being flexible enough to address problems and take advantage of opportunities.

STRATEGY 5. *Gain and maintain staff and client cooperation.*

Any field experiment (and most applied research) is headed for disaster if the evaluator fails to persuade the staff and residents of the need for doing it, the need for following the procedures, and the general ethics of the entire study. It is therefore essential to involve program staff throughout the planning, implementation, and analysis of field experiments. Some of the potential strategies that have been identified already (Boruch, Dennis, and Greer, 1988; Dennis, 1994; Dennis, 1988, 1994) for gaining and maintaining staff cooperation include the following:

Explain to the staff why the study is being done and how the information is going to be used. They need to be persuaded just like everyone else.

Present the draft instruments and procedures to the staff for their critique and input. They may not be able to tell you what to do, but they will almost always be right in what they tell you will cause a problem.

Be responsive to staff concerns and make some accommodations. Even if you cannot eliminate every problem raised by the staff (for example, more paperwork), accommodating them on some issues will make them more likely to go along in other areas.

Give the staff feedback on the study's progress and findings. Many experiments take several years. As in any endeavor, staff should be given pep talks. Let them know that you are actually using all of that extra paperwork and that their efforts are needed and appreciated.

Be sensitive to internal time horizons and deadlines. Minimize the extent to which your procedures and reporting guidelines conflict with the program's operations. Much of the information you will collect may have alternative uses by the program staff and should be shared where feasible.

Make staff leadership part of the research team. Their clinical insights will pay off in many unexpected ways.

The last two points can be very tricky. It is important to define whether program staff are collaborators with full access to the data or the subject of an independent evaluation. Although the latter may make some clients more willing to respond, it may make it more difficult to share or link the data later and can certainly limit their usefulness to the program. Whichever decision is made, it should be spelled out clearly in the informed consent process.

It is also important to understand that moving an intervention protocol from a manual to reality is rarely a smooth process. The more the staff leadership is involved and understands the intent of the intervention, the more they can help make the intervention become an intrinsic part of the program's daily operations. Training should try to anticipate and address potential barriers. There should be immediate follow-up to ensure that the intervention is initially implemented, as well as long-term follow-up training and feedback to maintain quality control. Ideally, the implementation should include integrating the intervention into existing systems (for example, organizational meetings, procedures) for routine quality control of the intervention protocol.

STRATEGY 6. *Minimize attrition to maximize the degree of internal validity.*

Even if a person drops out of an intervention, most studies will still want to conduct follow-up interviews. Failure to follow up 70 percent or more of the residents will make it almost impossible to publish the findings in the most respected journals or to disseminate the findings. Some of the ways that have been identified (Dennis, 1994; Howard, Krause, and Orlinsky, 1986) for preventing attrition include the following:

Explain the study thoroughly to the client and elicit a commitment. This may sound obvious, but many clients do not realize what they are committing to. For some clients, information about how the information will be used may also affect their commitment to the study, particularly if it can be related to something in which they have a vested interest.

Provide incentives for cooperation. Besides telling the client how the information will be used, it is often useful to offer monetary or token (food, toiletries) incentives for completing an interview and to even offer a separate incentive for scheduling and completing the interview on time.

Collect locator information. One of the most basic techniques is to collect information about the client and about other people who would know where to contact that client for a follow-up.

Stay in contact. Researchers are learning to stay in contact with clients, either indirectly through program staff or directly with telephone calls or postcards. Some studies provide incentives to clients for visiting the program, calling the program staff, or returning a postcard to the researchers. Longitudinal studies of homeless people are being done now and include incentives for the homeless person to regularly contact the researcher.

Use official records. Some of the more sophisticated tracking information sources include the Social Security Administration, state driver's license bureau, the National Death Registry, crime reports, and credit agencies.

Employ outreach workers. For hard-to-reach populations such as injection drug users or homeless people, many studies employ indigenous workers familiar with the client's community to help locate people who cannot otherwise be found for follow-up.

Give it time. With enough money and time, field staff can always find one more client. Although there is clearly a point of diminishing returns, the locating process should actively begin several weeks before the target date and continue as long as it is still cost-effective. Note that it is better to have an interview three weeks late and have to adjust for the time window than to have no data at all.

Although these procedures will not eliminate attrition, staff at RTI and other research institutes have used them to repeatedly obtain response rates from 75 percent to 95 percent even two to five after clients had left treatment.

Analysis. Both during the experiment and after it comes out of the field, the evaluator will be doing analyses. All too often, evaluators jump to the main analysis without considering the quality of the experiment or the extent to which the intervention was actually implemented. They also need to consider technical issues, such as the statistical power or sensitivity of the analysis model, how to deal with the problems that did occur, and how to interpret mixed or unexpected findings.

STRATEGY 7. *Assess the quality and validity of an experiment.*

Although applied research and field experiments have enormous potential impact on the field, they are clearly not without problems. Because even the best plan can go wrong, it is essential to assess the validity of an experiment before trying to interpret the outcomes. Some of the specific techniques that have been identified (Dennis, 1990, 1994) include the following:

Measure the actual amount and quality of treatment received by each client.
Compare treatment levels before and after the implementation of the randomized experiment in an interrupted time series design.
Compare the treatment received with the proposed level of treatment to measure compliance.
Carefully monitor random assignments to detect violations.
Monitor environmental changes and, where they are large, incorporate covariates for them into the analysis.
Incorporate planned intervention changes as either a covariate or change in dosage in the outcome analysis.

Although statistical issues must be addressed, we all too often overlook these equally important questions that influence our understanding of what was actually done.

STRATEGY 8. *Use more appropriate and sensitive analysis techniques.*

Given the likelihood of large individual differences and variation in the treatment implementation (by site, staff, and individual), it is essential that more statistically powerful methods be used in the analyses. These include repeated measures, analysis of variance (ANOVA), multiple regression, survival analysis, and structural equation modeling. It is critical to check for violations of the assumptions in field research and to try to use random effect or logistic models when they are closer to the actual phenomena being studied. Certainly, the more appropriate, valid, timely, reliable, and sensitive the measures are, the better. But given any specific measure, it is important to find the most sensitive and appropriate means to analyze the data.

To illustrate, let us consider a situation in which a service is offered as part of the experimental intervention, but only some residents take advantage of it. The intervention is therefore likely to change both the mean and variance (or range) of the treatment received and outcomes. Most statistical software will generate tests that assume that the variances are the same (except for chance) or use a formula that adjusts for independent samples (Snedecor and Cochran, 1989). The most common adjustment is to take the square root of the sum of the two variance estimates (each divided by its n) as shown in equation 1.

$$\text{Variance}_{\text{Adjusted}} = \text{SQRT (Standard Deviation}_1 / n_1 + \text{Standard Deviation}_2 / n_2) \tag{1}$$

Although this equation is clearly appropriate for a survey of two independent samples or for estimating the differences between two means, it will assume that any experimental impact on the variance was just noise and underrepresent the intervention's impact on the total distribution.

As an initial approach it is therefore often useful to start the analysis by calculating the effect size based on the control group only (Dennis, 1994). This is the parametric equivalent of a Wilcoxon–Mann–Whitney Rank Order test to see whether there has been a change in the total distribution (Siegel and Castellan, 1988). Equations 2 and 3 illustrate how the effect size with a pooled standard deviation is much smaller than that from a control deviation when the experimental intervention has had an effect on the variance.

$$\text{Effect size} = (\text{MEAN}_{\text{Experimental}} - \text{MEAN}_{\text{Control}}) = (3.63 - 2.54) / 4.19 = 1.09 / 4.19 = .26 / \text{Standard Deviation}_{\text{Pooled}} \tag{2}$$

$$\text{Effect size} = (\text{MEAN}_{\text{Experimental}} - \text{MEAN}_{\text{Control}}) = (3.63 - 2.54) / 3.41 = 1.09 / 3.41 = .40 / \text{Standard Deviation}_{\text{Control}} \tag{3}$$

Although the pooled and control group's standard deviation are the same under the null hypothesis used for statistical testing, they produce very different results. The latter increases the effect size by 54 percent (.40/.26) or, alternatively, decreases the required sample size for 80 percent power by 43 percent (108/251.5). If a difference is found between the distributions, then there are many standard tests for determining whether there are differences between the means, variances, or both (see Hayes, 1981).

STRATEGY 9. *Measure and be prepared to analyze noncompliance with random assignment.*

One of the few issues truly specific to randomized experiments is what to do when the client or staff person does not comply with random assignment. Some of the basic approaches to dealing with noncompliance include the following:

Assess the intervention's effect both as assigned and as delivered. Berk (1990), Berk and Sherman (1988), and Dennis (1990) argued for calculating the effect both ways to create an upper and lower bound of sorts.

Adjust the participation effect to inflate the treatment effect. Like a survey's nonresponse rate adjustment, the observed effect is divided by the fraction of people who participated. Bloom (1984) argued that this would represent the expected effect if everyone had participated.

Stratify conditions on the basis of the treatment received. Cook and Poole (1982) found that even crude measures of the treatment received (none/any) were capable of increasing the statistical power by more than 10 percent. Cook and Campbell (1979) recommended looking at the pre/post effect of groups with different dosages of treatment, expecting to see a fan-spread pattern if dosage is important.

Construct a discriminant function to predict treatment use among the experimental group, then subset both groups on the basis of the equation (regardless of actual treatment use). Vinokur, Price, and Caplan (1991) found that this approach could be used to construct a matched control group and estimate the effect of likely service users.

Although it is clearly better to avoid this problem, each of these approaches will ensure reasonable levels of acceptance in major journals and professional forums.

STRATEGY 10. *Put as much care into qualitative aspects of the research design as quantitative ones.*

In this context, previous debates between quantitative and qualitative research—in which experiments are often viewed as one or the other—can be seen as trivial. No randomized field experiment is likely to succeed or be useful without a lot of good qualitative work. Some of the junctures critical to the study's qualitative analysis include working with practitioners and clients to define the questions and develop meaningful interventions, explaining the intervention to the participants in a way that makes them willing to participate, carefully monitoring the actual implementation to detect unexpected problems or the need to refine the experiment, and working with practitioners and staff to identify and interpret key phenomena.

A comprehensive textbook is not currently available on the role of qualitative evaluation in the management of randomized field experiments, but such models as ethnographic auditing could be readily adapted for monitoring organizations in general (for a brief review, see Fetterman, 1990, and Fetterman, this volume).

One great mistake that is often made is to treat the qualitative analysis as though it were some kind of adjunct or substudy. Although rigorous methods and statistical tests should be used to evaluate theories, they do nothing to help develop the theories or identify what should be tested. A good qualitative analysis is one of the best ways to generate ideas to test and to formulate interpretations of what was observed. This principle is best summarized in a proverb used to teach the Egyptian pharaoh Ptahhotep the art of "good speak" (communication) from one of the oldest known books (circa 2388 B.C. to 2356 B.C.): "Do not be proud or arrogant with your knowledge. Consult and converse with the ignorant and the wise, for the limits of art are not reached. No artist ever possesses that perfection to which he should aspire. *Good speech* is more hidden than greenstone, yet it may be found among maids at the grindstones." (Hilliard, Williams, and Damali, 1987).

Conclusion

We have tried to identify several strategies that address common design, implementation, and analysis problems. The use of randomized experiments to evaluate real programs is feasible, but not without a wide range of methodological, logistical, managerial, and analytical challenges. Given the intensive level of human and organizational resources involved, it is ethically imperative that randomized field experiments be designed to serve multiple audiences and involve multiple levels of research design. This concept merely recognizes that, in the real world, program managers and policy-makers are rarely interested in answering just a single question or serving only the "average" or "model" client. Their varied clients present problems that require more complex solutions.

References

Bentler, P. M. "Modeling of Intervention Effects." In C. G. Leukefeld and W. J. Bukoski (eds.), *Drug Abuse Prevention Intervention Research: Methodological Issues.* NIDA Research Monograph 107, DHHS Publication No. ADM 91–1761. Rockville, Md.: National Institute on Drug Abuse, 1991, pp. 159–82.

Berk, R. A. *What Your Mother Never Told You About Randomly Controlled Trials* (No. 44 in the UCLA Statistic Series). Unpublished report available from the author. Los Angeles: Department of Sociology and Program in Social Statistics, University of California, Los Angeles, 1990.

Berk, R. A., and Sherman, L. W. "Police Response to Family Violence Incidents: An Analysis of an Experimental Design with Incomplete Randomization." *Journal of the American Statistical Association,* 1988, *83* (401), 70–76.

Berk, R. A., and others. "Social Policy Experimentation: A Position Paper." *Evaluation Review,* 1985, *9,* 387–429.

Blalock, H. M. (ed.). *Causal Models in Panel and Experimental Designs.* New York: Aldine, 1985.

Bloom, H. S. "Accounting for No-Shows in Experimental Evaluation Designs." *Evaluation Review,* 1984, *8,* 225–46.

Boruch, R. F. "On Common Contentions about Randomized Field Experiments." In G. V. Glass (ed.), *Evaluation Studies Review Annual.* Beverly Hills, Calif.: Sage, 1976, pp. 158–94.

Boruch, R. F. "Conducting Social Policy Experiments. In D. S. Cordray, S. Bloom, and R. J. Light (eds.), *Evaluation Practice in Review.* New Directions in Program Evaluation, no. 34. San Francisco: Jossey-Bass, 1987, pp. 45–66.

Boruch, R. F., Dennis, M. L., and Greer, K. C. "Lessons from the Rockefeller Foundation's Experiments on the Minority Female Single Parent Program." *Evaluation Review,* 1988, *12,* 396–42.

Campbell, D. T., and Stanley, J. S. "Experimental and Quasi-Experimental Designs for Research on Teaching." In N. L. Gage (ed.), *Handbook of Research on Teaching.* Chicago: Rand McNally, 1963.

Cook, T. D., and Campbell, D. *Quasi-Experimentation: Design and Analysis Issues for Field Settings.* Boston: Houghton-Mifflin, 1979.

Cook, T. J., and Poole, W. K. "Treatment Implementation and Statistical Power: A Research Note." *Evaluation Review,* 1982, *6,* 425–30.

Dennis, M. L. *Implementing Randomized Field Experiments: An Analysis of Criminal and Civil Justice Research.* Unpublished doctoral dissertation, Northwestern University, Evanston, Ill., 1988.

Dennis, M. L. "Assessing the Validity of Randomized Field Experiments: An Example from Drug Abuse Treatment Research." *Evaluation Review,* 1990, *14* (4), 347–73.

Dennis, M. L. "Ethical and Practical Randomized Field Experiments." In J. S. Wholey, H. Hatry, and K. Newcomber (eds.), *Handbook of Practical Program Evaluation.* San Francisco: Jossey-Bass, 1994, pp. 155–197.

Dennis, M. L., and Boruch, R. F. "Randomized Experiments for Planning and Testing Projects in Developing Countries: Threshold Conditions." *Evaluation Review,* 1989, *13,* 292–309.

Dennis, M. L., Fairbank, J. A., and Rachal, J. V. "Measuring Substance Abuse Counseling." Paper presented at the 100th Annual Conference of the American Psychological Association, Washington, D.C., August 1992.

Dennis, M. L., and others. "Developing a Training and Employment Programs to Meet the Needs of Methadone Treatment Clients." *Evaluation and Program Planning,* 1993, *16,* 73–86.

Donner, A., Birkett, N., and Buck, C. "Randomization by Cluster: Sample Size Requirements and Analysis." *American Journal of Epidemiology,* 1981, *114,* 283–86.

Donner, A., and Donald, A. "The Analysis of Data Arising from a Stratified Design with the Cluster as Unit of Randomization." *Statistics in Medicine,* 1987, *6,* 43–52.

Efron, B., and Feldman, D. "Compliance as an Explanatory Variable in Clinical Trials." *Journal of the American Statistical Association,* 1991, *86* (413), 9–17.

Fairweather, G. W., and Tornatzky, L. G. *Experimental Methods for Social Policy Research.* New York: Pergamon Press, 1977.

Federal Judicial Center. *Experimentation in the Law: Report of the Federal Judicial Center Advisory Committee on Experimentation in the Law.* Washington, D.C.: Federal Judicial Center, 1981.

Fetterman, D. M. "Ethnographic Auditing: A New Approach to Evaluating Management." In W. G. Tierney (ed.), *Assessing Academic Climates and Cultures.* New Directions for Institutional Research, no. 68. San Francisco: Jossey-Bass, 1990, pp. 19–34.

Fisher, R. A. *The Design of Experiments.* (7th ed.) New York: Hafner, 1960.

Fuller, R. K., and others. "Disulfiram Treatment of Alcoholism." *Journal of the American Medical Association,* 1986, *245,* 1449–55.

Hayes, W. L. *Statistics.* (3rd ed.) New York: Holt, Rinehart, and Winston, 1981.

Hilliard, A. G., Williams, L., and Damali, N. (eds.). *The Teaching of Ptahhotep: The Oldest Book in the World.* Atlanta, Ga.: Blackwood Press, 1987.

Howard, K. I., Krause, M. S., and Orlinsky, D. E. "The Attrition Dilemma: Towards a New Strategy for Psychotherapy Research." *Journal of Consulting and Clinical Psychology,* 1986, *54,* 106–110.

Lipsey, M. W. *Design Sensitivity: Statistical Power for Experimental Research.* Newbury Park, Calif.: Sage, 1990.

Renner, B., and Sechrest, L. "Experimental Research in Therapeutic Communities." Paper presented at the annual meeting of the American Evaluation Association, November 5–7, Seattle, Wash., 1992.

Research Triangle Institute. *Software for Survey Data Analysis (SUDAAN), Version 5.30.* Research Triangle Park, N.C.: Research Triangle Institute, 1991.

Riecken, H. W., and others. *Social Experimentation: A Method for Planning and Evaluating Social Programs.* New York: Academic Press, 1974.

Saxe, L., and Fine, M. *Social Experiments: Methods for Design and Evaluation.* Sage Library of Social Research, Vol. 131. Beverly Hills, Calif.: Sage, 1981.

Siegel, S., and Castellan, N. J. *Nonparametric Statistics for the Behavioral Sciences.* (2nd ed.) New York: McGraw-Hill, 1988.

Snedecor, G. W., and Cochran, W. G. *Statistical Methods.* (8th ed.) Ames: Iowa State University Press, 1989.

Vinokur, A. D., Price, R. H., and Caplan, R. D. "From Field Experiments to Program Implementation: Assessing the Potential Outcomes of an Experimental Intervention Program for Unemployed Persons." *American Journal of Community Psychology,* 1991, *19,* 543–62.

Wallace, L. W. "The Community Penalties Act of 1983: An Evaluation of the Law, Its Implementation, and Its Impact in North Carolina." Unpublished doctoral dissertation. Lincoln: University of Nebraska, 1987.

MICHAEL L. DENNIS is senior research psychologist in the Center for Social Research and Policy Analysis at the Research Triangle Institute, Research Triangle Park, North Carolina.

ROBERT F. BORUCH is an endowed chair of measurement and evaluation in the School of Education at the University of Pennsylvania, Philadelphia.

The atmosphere is changing as we examine the real-world prob-
lems associated with the implementation of the experimental
design.

Keeping Research on Track

David M. Fetterman

These stories are riveting. Reading these stories is like watching a train wreck. Experimental designs resemble railroad tracks—strong iron bars guiding a powerful locomotive from station to station. However, this image of technological power and precision is an illusion. The ease with which this type of research train is derailed at every turn is evident from each of these reports. I have ridden these tracks myself.

Over a decade ago, I published an article titled "Ibsen's Baths: Reactivity and Insensitivity (A Misapplication of the Treatment-Control Design in a National Evaluation)" (Fetterman 1982). It generated considerable discussion and a fair amount of heat, and it also shed some light on this topic. The article described a misapplication of the experimental design in educational research and raised ethical concerns about applying this design to primarily low-income minority high school dropouts. In an alternative high school for dropouts, young adults who were assigned to the control group were intentionally deprived of a benefit (a program based on an exemplary prototype). Moreover, they were being denied a second chance to function productively within the system. The effects of turning away an individual whose desire to lead a productive life has been rekindled are numerous and profound. Interviews with rejected students and their parents confirmed the deleterious effects of this approach to research.

The implementation of this design—much like the examples described in this collection—was methodologically bankrupt. In this national evaluation, one segment of a biased sample was placed in the treatment group (individuals who were not turned off by the rigorous examination and lottery system) and another segment, according to parents, were "slapped in the face"—told they could not enter the program. The second group represented the control group. In fact, there was no control group, merely a negative treatment or reactive control group to be compared to a biased sample of treatment students. The problem was further compounded by the Hawthorne (Roethlisberger and Dickson, 1939) and John Henry effects (Saretsky, 1972), and by the problems of differential attrition in both treatment and control groups.

The most serious programmatic problems generated by this design concerned recruitment. Program staff members faced an uphill battle to sell a program to potential students and their parents who considered it a risk, primarily because it was a demonstration program. When program staff members added that admission was further predicated on the students' luck in being chosen by lottery, the appeal of the program was more than slightly tarnished.

The implementation of this design generated additional programmatic obstacles in the area of recruitment. The professional testers were initially instructed not to test potential students unless fifteen or more students could be identified for testing at the sites. Consequently, staff members were unable to inform many students when testing would occur. Students waiting for about four weeks lost interest in the program. The attrition rates between the initial interview and testing ranged from 26 to 59 percent.

The parallels between these abbreviated examples and the ones described in this collection are not accidental or remarkable. They are directly related to this research design. The key difference lies in the reaction to these discussions. A decade ago, I encountered passionate resistance to the discussion of the misuse of a paradigm fundamental to educational research. (See Fetterman 1982.) I argued that the evaluation relied on information drawn from a misapplication of the treatment-control design. (The resistance this generated among other researchers was ultimately harmful to the individuals they sought to assist.) The article also examines the real-world constraints and views of the federal bureaucracy, the research corporation, and the educational research establishment to explain why policy-makers and researchers continue using this design.

This collection proves that the atmosphere has changed. Instead of being perceived as attacking a sacred cow, colleagues are able—without censure—to critically and openly examine the real-world problems associated with the implementation of the experimental design. An open climate is essential to build on our knowledge base and to determine when it is and is not appropriate to use this design and how to implement it appropriately and effectively, minimizing reactivity and insensitivity. I applaud the authors in this collection for presenting an engaging examination of their work. Clearly, progress is being made.

The challenge ahead is to keep this open and frank self-examination alive and focused. This collection provides a clear focus on real problems. It also begins a constructive discussion about preventive measures and solutions. However, we need to hear more stories of creative solutions to these problems. Although many technical problems need to be resolved, the underlying problems are not power analyses but insensitivities that can and must be addressed.

It is not our job to go along for the ride. We have an obligation to try to keep the train on track. It is also within our power to control the speed with which this locomotive is barreling down the track and our responsibility to determine the destination of this journey.[1]

Note

1. See Fetterman 1993 for a series of examples demonstrating how researchers are trying to keep the research train on track as they address a host of significant issues including environmental health and safety, the student dropout problem, educational reform, AIDS education, homelessness, conflict resolution, American Indian concerns, and the education of gifted and talented children.

References

Fetterman, D. M. "Ibsen's Baths: Reactivity and Insensitivity (A Misapplication of the Treatment-Control Design in a National Evaluation)." *Educational Evaluation and Policy Analysis,* 1982, *4* (3), 261–79.

Fetterman, D. M. *Speaking the Language of Power: Communication, Collaboration, and Advocacy (Translating Ethnography into Action).* London, England: Falmer Press, 1993.

Roethlisberger, F. J., and Dickson, W. J. *Management and the Worker.* Cambridge, Mass.: Harvard University Press, 1939.

Saretsky, G. "The OEO P.C. Experiment and the John Henry Effect." *Phi Delta Kappan,* 1972, *53,* 579–81.

DAVID M. FETTERMAN *is former president of the American Evaluation Association. He is a professor and research director at the California Institute of Integral Studies and a member of the professoriat and the director of the M.A. Policy Analysis Program at Stanford University.*

Index

Lam, J. A., 11, 13, 14, 20, 21, 67, 78, 79
Larntz, K., 74
Leaf, P. J., 55, 68
Leakage, 27, 75, 80, 81
Levitan, S. A., 5
Lifeboat effect. *See also* Gender bias
Lipsey, M., 71, 87, 90
Lyons, J. S., 2, 3, 16, 23

McAuliffe, W. E., 5, 10, 13, 14, 20, 21, 74
McLellan, A. T., 32, 35
Manning, M., 17
Manpower Demonstration Research Corporation (MDRC), 12
Mark, M. M., 20
Martinez, A., 55
Mesch, B., 68
Messick, S., 7
Miller, T. Q., 16
Minority clients, possible exploitation of, 56. *See also* Gender bias
Mono-operation bias, 12
Mono-method bias, 19
Motivation and readiness for treatment, 76
Mullen, R., 46
Multiple life problems, 42

National Death Registry, 95
National Institute of Justice (NIJ), 87
National Institute on Alcohol Abuse and Alcoholism (NIAAA), 16, 23, 46, 55, 56, 64, 69, 70, 73, 74
National Institute on Drug Abuse (NIDA), 46, 55, 73
Needs assessment, 84
New Haven Project, 55–66; *See also* GSP organizational problems in, 67–72.
New Orleans Substance Abusers Program (NOHSAP), 28–40; actual randomization of clients, 33–37; client characteristics, 29; equivalence between groups, 35; experimental efficacy of, 33; Extended Care/Independent living (ECIL) program, 28–29; gender bias in, 35–37; intervention model of, 28–29; program staff and research staff conflict, 30; selection of clients for treatment, 28, 30; staff resistance to randomization, 30–40; Transitional Care (TC) program, 28–29; treatment goals and intervention philosophy of, 28
NIAAA, 46, 55, 56, 64, 69, 70, 73, 74
NIAAA Cooperative Agreement, 73

NIDA, 46, 55, 73
NOHSAP, 27, 28–40
Nonrandom selection factor, 33
Norcross, J. C., 17

Oasis, 51
Orlinsky, D. E., 95
Orwin, R. G., 5, 11, 16, 23, 85

Parikh, G., 33, 35
Payment for participation, 60–61
Pilot tests of randomization, 76–77
Pipeline studies, 74–76; generalizability issues and, 76
Placement of dependent children, 46–47; parental motivation and, 47; visitation and, 51. *See also* Gender bias
Policy, implications of, 52–54
Polysubstance abuse, 29
Poole, W. K., 98
Postward monitoring, 84
Preaward site visits, 83–84
Price, R. H., 98
Probability samples, 27
Prochaska, J. O., 17
Program-research conflict, 32

Rachal, J. V., 87
Random irrelevancies, 12
Randomization: acceptance of, by staff, 46–49; assignment of couples and, 50–51; client self-organization, effects on, 51; community concerns and, 56, 68–72; community service providers, impact on, 61–63; demoralization caused by, 60; differential attrition rate, in ASSET, and, 51; emotional dilemmas and, 31, 42, 67–72; feasibility studies for, 45; gender-based selection bias and, 35–37, 47, 49; implementation of, 31–33, 73–86; internal validity and, 53, 68; New Haven Project and, 55–66, 67–72; NOHSAP clients, of, 33–37; NOHSAP design and, 29–39; NOHSAP staff resistance to, 30–40; vs. other designs, 47; parallel between surveys and, in experiments, 27; participant attitudes toward, 48; payment for participation and, 60–61; pilot tests of, 76–77; presentation of, to clients, 49; procedures, centralized control of, 77–78; process of, changing, 63–64; questions and concerns about, of

ORDERING INFORMATION

NEW DIRECTIONS FOR PROGRAM EVALUATION is a series of paperback books that presents the latest techniques and procedures for conducting useful evaluation studies of all types of programs. Books in the series are published quarterly in Spring, Summer, Fall, and Winter and are available for purchase by subscription as well as by single copy.

SUBSCRIPTIONS for 1994 cost $54.00 for individuals (a savings of 34 percent over single-copy prices) and $75.00 for institutions, agencies, and libraries. Please do not send institutional checks for personal subscriptions. Standing orders are accepted.

SINGLE COPIES cost $17.95 when payment accompanies order. (California, New Jersey, New York, and Washington, D.C., residents please include appropriate sales tax.) Billed orders will be charged postage and handling.

DISCOUNTS FOR QUANTITY ORDERS are available. Please write to the address below for information.

ALL ORDERS must include either the name of an individual or an official purchase order number. Please submit your order as follows:
  Subscriptions: specify series and year subscription is to begin
  Single copies: include individual title code (such as PE59)

MAIL ALL ORDERS TO:
  Jossey-Bass Publishers
  350 Sansome Street
  San Francisco, California 94104-1342

FOR SUBSCRIPTION SALES OUTSIDE OF THE UNITED STATES, CONTACT:
  any international subscription agency or Jossey-Bass directly.

OTHER TITLES AVAILABLE IN THE
NEW DIRECTIONS FOR PROGRAM EVALUATION SERIES
William R. Shadish, Editor-in-Chief